IMAGES
of America

ROUTE 66
IN CALIFORNIA

"Temple" of the Four-Level Interchange. A great road-building accomplishment, the 110 (our own Arroyo Seco/Route 66 Parkway) intersects with the 101 very close to the Los Angeles Civic Center. As late as the 1960s, when this intriguing night shot was taken, city hall was still downtown's tallest building. It is now dwarfed in the skyline by skyscrapers on at least two sides. Here, though, the art deco tower almost appears to hold vigil over the angels and demons of the freeways. The upper-level spans leading into downtown are the 101 (Hollywood Freeway) and the 110, in the foreground, below. (Courtesy Pasadena Museum of History Archives.)

IMAGES
of America

ROUTE 66
IN CALIFORNIA

Glen Duncan and the California
Route 66 Preservation Foundation

ARCADIA
PUBLISHING

Published by Arcadia Publishing
Charleston, South Carolina

Printed in the United States of America

Library of Congress Catalog Card Number: 2005929103

For all general information contact Arcadia Publishing at:
Telephone 843-853-2070
Fax 843-853-0044
E-mail sales@arcadiapublishing.com
For customer service and orders:
Toll-Free 1-888-313-2665

Visit us on the Internet at www.arcadiapublishing.com

JOSHUA TREES. This quintessential scene of the California desert and mountains exemplifies one of the big attractions and pleasures of the trip out west for many 66ers. The juxtaposition of mountain snow and desert has an allure that transcends history. How many families across the country or the world have snapshots of scenes like this in albums of trips across Southern California? (Courtesy Seaver Center for Western History Research, Natural History Museum of Los Angeles County.)

CONTENTS

ACKNOWLEDGMENTS

One can never be sure that listing contributors to any idea or creative endeavor is ever really complete or thorough. I am nonetheless cognizant of the huge impact several people have had in building and stoking my interest in the history, culture, and economic importance of Route 66 in California.

At the top of the list is Jim Conkle, founder and executive director of the California Route 66 Preservation Foundation. Jim's commitment to and passion for the road is without par or precedent, and his enthusiasm and storytelling gift is almost impossible to resist. I am also indebted to many people and organizations in Pasadena and South Pasadena who have inspired, led, and renewed my enthusiasm for history and cultural heritage. They include Sue Mossman and a whole lot of people at Pasadena Heritage; Clarice Knapp, Joanne Nuckols, Rick Thomas, and dozens of volunteers on the South Pasadena Preservation Foundation and Cultural Heritage Commission who have set high-water marks in preservation service.

Two writers who blazed the trail and whose work greatly assisted this pictorial history deserve special mention. Vivian Davies put together the first publication on the path of Route 66 across California, providing mileage calibrations on its landmarks and history. Scott Piotrowski's colorful and informative book did a great job of delineating various alignments that evolved in urban Los Angeles as highway planners tried to cope with population increases and tourist traffic. Both publications are listed in the Bibliography on page 128.

Special thanks also to Michael Taylor and Kaisa Barthuli of the Route 66 Corridor Preservation Program in Santa Fe, New Mexico. Their work on behalf and in support of volunteer preservationists and road enthusiasts in all eight states along the Mother Road is absolutely fantastic. This book would not have been possible, though, without the generous assistance of many historians, curators and archivists in museums and libraries along California Route 66 who provided archival photographs and documentation. They include Carolyn Kozo Cole, Los Angeles Public Library; Steve Smith, Mojave River Valley Museum; Chick Kirk, California Route 66 Museum in Victorville; Lian Partlow, Pasadena Museum of History; Ho Nguyen, Santa Monica Historical Society; John Cahoon, Seaver Center for Western History Research, Los Angeles County Natural History Museum; John Anicic, Fontana Historical Society; Irwin Margiloff, Duarte Historical Society; Dennis Casebier, Mojave Desert Heritage and Cultural Association; and Morgan Yates, Automobile Club of Southern California Archives.

Thanks also to Arcadia Publishing authors John Anthony Adams; Nick Cataldo; Pat Krig and Barbara Van Houten; John David Landers; Mark Langill; Portia Lee and Jeff Samudio; and Paula Scott for generously allowing use of photographs from their books. I also have benefited greatly from able fact-checking assistance and advice of Vivian Davies, Jeff Samudio, and Charlie Fisher. Thanks to all of you.

And finally, I thank my wife, Pat, always an ardent supporter of every new venture, even though each endeavor has meant less time for her or for completing all the unfinished projects around the house.

INTRODUCTION

History of the transportation corridor across Southern California easily predates the history of Route 66. As trappers and explorers chose routes earlier used by indigenous tribes, so did successive waves of settlers arriving by wagon train. Railroads likewise followed paths of least resistance with access to water and necessary materials. For the same reason, the Route 66 roadbed cut its way pretty much parallel to the rail line, especially at first. With improving automobile and road-building technology, though, the line of asphalt became straighter, because passenger cars and heavy trucks could negotiate steeper ascents and thus were not forced to take the gentlest slopes across mountain terrains in the Mojave Desert.

To be sure, what began with Spanish explorers and was fueled by discovery of gold and silver continued to gain momentum with completion of transcontinental railroads and fascination with California as an agricultural and vacation paradise that had already gained momentum prior to the fin de siécle. Great tourist hotels, vast orchards, and vineyards dotted the Southern California countryside south of Cajon Pass. The real explosion, however, was set off by completion of coast-to-coast automobile routes. The leitmotif of this migration, this picking up stakes for a new start, was a multiethnic, multicultural adaptation to the needs and potential of the Southern California land and climate. It called out to Japanese fisherman and truck farmers; Italian grape growers and winemakers; Mexican vaqueros and field workers; Chinese merchants and laborers; and health- and wealth-seekers of every stripe, religion, and background.

A bronze plaque recently installed at the base of the new Chinatown gate at Broadway and Cesar Chavez expresses the sentiments of one of these ethnic groups:

> We came from far away, crossing the ocean to seek our dreams; together we have worked to create our new homeland. Hundred[s of] years of success were brought about by our forefathers; Continual prosperity relies on our children from generation to generation, Blue skies and blooming flowers can be seen everywhere; But these roots in Chinatown are forever the heart of our family.

Very much the same emotion, expanded beyond Chinatown, could apply to many other ethnic communities in Los Angeles and to hundreds of thousands of families who came west on Route 66, following their dreams and seeking better lives.

The 20th century brought a flourishing of California "automania" and the glitzy, golden era of Hollywood and magnificent movie palaces. At about this same time came establishment of U.S. Highway 66 on the National Old Trails route, the Jazz Age, and ordeals of crossing the desert during dust-bowl era migration. The road also played a big role in wartime military buildup and logistics, with training installations across the desert. The postwar 1950s and 1960s brought its greatest popularity, with widespread family vacation travel and the population explosion in Southern California.

Once completed, Route 66 itself was a common avenue of entry, commerce, and communication. Its direct and indirect contribution to tourism and visitor services and attraction of California to travelers from all around the world continues to this day. Yet even more critical to the state's cultural, social, and economic evolution are the commerce and the communities that have sprung up along the corridor, dependent on the parallel ribbons of road and rail for personnel, communication, and support. At various times, the roadside viewscape included square mile upon square mile of citrus groves, vineyards, military installations and training centers, film and television studios, colleges and universities, hospitals, parks, and playgrounds.

The Road as a Cultural Icon

Route 66 has a mystique unparalleled anywhere in the world. Fan clubs for the storied road have reportedly been formed in every developed country in the world. Tour operators in several countries organize and promote trips specifically for travelers eager to experience Route 66 America.

One might easily ask why. It's not the oldest highway from the east of the Mississippi to the West Coast. It's not the longest. It didn't even start from New York or Boston or Washington, D.C. on the East Coast. So why is the Route 66 sign one of the world's best known icons? Perhaps the early hyperbole designed to attract tourists and new residents to Southern California played a part. Having America's most popular homespun hero, Will Rogers, dub it "America's Main Street" didn't hurt. John Steinbeck pulled our heartstrings in chronicling experiences along what he called the "Mother Road" in *Travels with Charley* and *The Grapes of Wrath* (which became a major motion picture). Bobby Troupe, Nat King Cole, and a host of recording artists added a lighthearted invitation to "Get your Kicks on Route 66."

Then in the 1960s, as superhighways were beginning to prevail in long-distance travel, a CBS television series came along to plant seeds of rebirth, dramatizing "Route 66" road trip encounters of two guys in a Corvette in America's heartland. Such intimate contact with people and communities is rare in today's high-speed world of cookie-cutter tract houses and chain-store franchises for food, gas, and places to lay your head. Route 66, for many Americans and travelers from abroad, has simply become a signpost for a longing to return to that earlier, simpler pace and time.

Although stateside auto-tourism along the Route 66 corridor continues to grow, operators of significant roadside attractions along the Mother Road often report that nearly half or more of visitors in the summer travel season are from Europe and Asia. This photo-documentary seeks to provide a glimpse into the California portion of the culture that gives rise to this interest, a vicarious, time-warp trip into the road mystique.

It also links those of us who live in Southern California to our roots. Without much difficulty, most everyone living here today can trace our families back to someplace else. The majority of our families came sometime in the 20th century. And before the 1970s, most came via Route 66.

End of the Rainbow: Making the Trip Worth the While

Perhaps more than any place in the eight states along its route, Southern California was a destination. This did not happen by accident. Beginning in the late 1800s, when railroads and major tourist hotels hired prominent artists and writers to picture and extol the virtues of Southern California living, boosterism has played a huge role in attracting visitors and new residents. At the beginning of the age of personalized motoring, the Automobile Club of Southern California jumped headlong into the game, not just as a travel promoter, but as a primary advocate for a superb road system for people to travel on once they got here. The club also had an aggressive program of posting signs and distributing maps across the country, directing travelers how to find their way to the promised panoply of tourist wonders. In those early days, Los Angeles was indeed a long and sometime arduous trek for travelers from the East and Midwest. Bad as the roads were then, as compared even to the two-lane blacktop era of the 1940s, 1950s, and 1960s, this corridor had the distinct advantage of being open year-round. The Auto Club, in fact, deserves a lot of the credit for Route 66 being here at all.

Southern California was certainly not the only Route 66 objective. Chicago, St Louis, Tulsa, the Grand Canyon and hundreds of locations, large and small, were destinations in their own right for millions of travelers. But the lure of the Southwest, particularly in the winter months, to people in northeastern and midwestern population centers, combined with the variety of Southern California tourist opportunities, made Los Angeles the end of the Route 66 rainbow for countless travelers. One could take other routes south to San Diego or north to San Francisco (and many did), but you couldn't go further on the Mother Road, except to go back home (and many did not).

DOCUMENTARY PERSPECTIVE

Capturing and documenting the essence of this history along a 350-mile or so stretch of asphalt, which in several places changed course several times over the years, turned out to be a more difficult task than anticipated. Decisions about what images and facets of the Route 66 story to include resulted in an early scrapping of an initial chronological outline because it didn't easily show the transformations that have taken place in communities along the road. On the other hand, a strict "then vs. now" format also was not easily accomplished because many of the necessary historical pictures were simply not available. Either of these presentation styles also would have directed the focus away from what is really special about the history and culture of Route 66 in California.

What we set out to provide, instead, is a look at the special history of U.S. Highway 66 across Southern California, how it came to be, why people came out here, what they came to see, and what still endures. We focused more on the spirit and culture of the road rather than being limited to a strict adherence to chronology or to changes in transportation and roadside architecture.

In assembling the pictures, though, I found myself wishing for access to photographs that may in fact never have been taken or searching for printable original copies of newspaper and magazine images that had long since disappeared. I ardently sought images of Route 66 travelers on the road enjoying California roadside conveniences and regional attractions, with names, dates, and comments about their experiences. Many thousands of these images and remembrances are surely stored away in countless shoe boxes and family albums all across the country. Hopefully, someday we might be able to post a selection of these on our California Route 66 Preservation Foundation website (http://www.cart66pf.org).

Unfortunately, "Kodak moments" never captured Native American life on the old Mojave trail or travails of pioneers who followed in their steps. Missing also are images of the monumental effort of the Automobile Club of Southern California in building and maintaining the National Old Trails Road and providing signage and maps to guide travelers out here.

Another challenge was deciding whether to limit the viewpoint to resources actually on the roadside (e.g., addresses on a street or road during a period in which Route 66 was so aligned) or to take a broader view to include common side trips and tourist destinations of Route 66 travelers in various periods of significance. We chose the latter point of view for this photo-documentary. Other books and Route 66 travel guides that focus on roadside conveniences are already available, and more are likely in the future. A comprehensive historic resource survey is also underway that will document in substantial detail all historic resources on all alignments of the California corridor.

Thus we see tourist attractions of Santa Monica and Venice long before Route 66 actually went that far and, in fact, never did go all the way to the Ocean or Santa Monica Pier. Few tourists who came all the way from the East or Midwest before or after 1936 (when the route was extended from Downtown Los Angeles to Lincoln Avenue in Santa Monica) would have skipped the chance to dip their toes in the Pacific Ocean. Likewise, from the time Disneyland opened in 1955, it was a primary destination for millions of Route 66 travelers, although a good hour's drive south of Route 66's course through downtown Los Angeles.

Many other facets of the California Route 66 experience also became part of the story, even if the best examples were not tied to addresses on the road. These include Depression-era hardships and accommodations; wartime mobilization and cultural changes; the movie and television industries and fascination with Hollywood celebrities; and the exotic blend of scenery, featuring snow-capped mountains, desert flora, and sparkling beaches.

This freedom from having to tie each image to its location on the route, or to a particular period of significance (i.e., "When did the road pass by this location?") allowed a fuller and more complete focus on Route 66 culture as it contributed to California history and development. And perhaps even more important, it permitted us to witness how the aura and attraction of Route 66 may itself have been shaped by the uniqueness of Southern California destinations and attractions.

A great majority of the images are nonetheless actually along the Route 66 roadside. The premise we followed in selecting images and presenting the text was that, like the Route 66 mystique, the links between road and what we attend to are often more a matter of interest than distances on a map or historic periods of significance. Most of us had no problem with the fact that very few of the episodes of the *Route 66* television series took place in communities along U.S. Highway 66. But the forays of Todd and Buzz into America's heartland captured one of the core distinctions of Route 66 travel that we have almost lost in this era of high-speed interstates and long-distance travel 35,000 feet above the road—the chance to experience America.

What we have here, then, is a chance to time-travel the California Route 66 experience, courtesy of photo-archivists from communities along its path. The embarkation point is a brief section on the road's prehistory, followed by a historically annotated, multi-era trip across Southern California from Needles to Santa Monica, with side trips to many of the things that brought travelers out here.

One

ROUTE 66 PREHISTORY

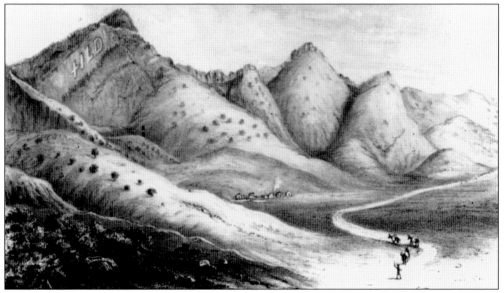

THE OLD MOJAVE TRAIL. Although neither artist nor location of this charcoal drawing is known, it depicts the kind of environment the earliest western adventurers and prospectors might have experienced along the old Mojave Trail in the early 1800s. And that trail would have been predated, perhaps by hundreds of years, by Native American footpaths that led west to the ocean. (Courtesy Mojave River Valley Museum.)

THEN CAME THE PIONEERS. Following the same trails blazed in bygone eras, and which would be followed many years later by the Santa Fe Railroad, the National Old Trails Road, and U.S. Highway 66, pioneer settlers made the arduous trek across the Mojave Desert with whatever family and possessions that could survive the trip. (Courtesy Mojave River Valley Museum.)

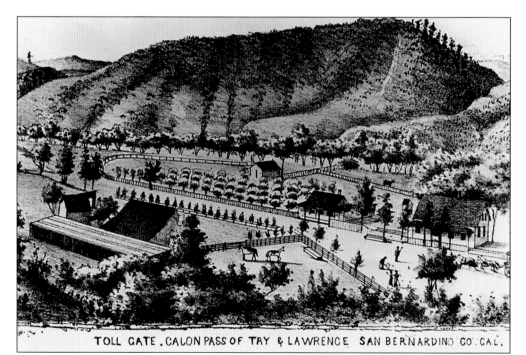

TOLL GATE. CAJON PASS OF TAY & LAWRENCE SAN BERNARDINO CO. CAL.

CAJON PASS AND THE MORMON TOLL GATE. By the late 19th century, Mormon settlers had improved the wagon trail over Cajon Pass. There were two toll gates, one near the bottom of the graded dirt roadway and one at the summit. Travelers at that time were only too happy to pay for use of the improved route, open year-round, from the high desert down to San Bernardino. (Courtesy Mojave River Valley Museum.)

HODGES RETURN HOME OVER CAJON PASS. This 1911 photograph shows Robert and Gilbert Hodge hauling supplies from San Bernardino over what we would now call an "unimproved road." In that day and age, this one was a good deal better than many. The family, early settlers in the area north of Victorville, founded the town of Hodge. (Courtesy Mojave River Valley Museum.)

NATIONAL OLD TRAILS ROAD. The scene here at the Melrose Hotel in Barstow is of an Automobile Club of Southern California service truck being greeted by local movers and shakers. The great distance between Los Angeles and major Eastern and Midwestern cities virtually required good roads, signage, and maps to capture tourists and investment. So the Automobile Club of Southern California took on these tasks and, with a healthy dose of civic booster-ism, the club began posting signs and distributing maps to help motorists find their ways from as far east as Kansas City. The eventual goal was to take the program all the way to New York City. By 1914, when signage was completed between Albuquerque and L.A., the club magazine extolled its "thousand-mile invitation" to the eastern motorist to visit Southern California. (Courtesy Mojave River Valley Museum.)

Two

MOJAVE DESERT
COLORADO RIVER TO BARSTOW

COLORADO RIVER, NEEDLES. A view of the Colorado River below the site for Hoover Dam, this photograph was taken *c.* 1934. The Needles peaks appear in the background. (Courtesy Security Pacific Collection, Los Angeles Public Library.)

The Road into California, 1948. Red Rock Bridge, in the foreground, was formerly a railroad span but was converted to highway use in 1947. Before that, the Mother Road had used the old arch bridge in the background. The Red Rock Bridge was dismantled in 1976, 10 years after Interstate 40 led to the closure of this part of Route 66 over the Colorado River at Topock, just south of Needles, California. (Courtesy Vivian Davies.)

Snow in Needles. In summer, Needles often has the distinction of recording some of the hottest temperatures in the country. Winters are usually very comfortable, but on January 12, 1949, when this picture was taken in front of the El Garces train station and Harvey House, it was a bit chilly. The El Garces, one of the premiere stations on the Santa Fe Line, is listed on the National Register of Historic Places and, hopefully, is destined for restoration and reuse. It's a fabulous old "Queen of the Road" and gave rail travelers and motorists a royal welcome into California. (Courtesy Mojave River Valley Museum.)

66 Motel. Simple and direct, this historic motel sign still pulls 'em in, although the facility is now rented by the week or month. (Courtesy Route 66 Corridor Preservation Program, National Park Service.)

PALMS MOTEL, NEEDLES, 1950. The Palms, a successful tourist court from the 1920s, is still in business. This shot is more or less on the way out of town. Needles was the hub of railroad and river transportation for several decades, particularly during World War II. (Courtesy Vivian Davies.)

WHITE COTTAGE RESTAURANT. The restaurant was right along the National Old Trails Road and the earliest alignment of Route 66. Goffs Schoolhouse, now listed on the National Register, is in the background. The schoolhouse was constructed in 1914 to teach the children of families who came to the region to mine, ranch, and build railroads and highways. The school continued until 1937, when a newer one was built in Essex. (Courtesy Dennis Casebier, Mojave Desert Archives, Goffs, California.)

GOFFS SCHOOLHOUSE. The old schoolhouse has been completely and lovingly restored. It now serves as the Mojave Desert Heritage and Cultural Center. In its heyday, Goffs (elevation 2,700 feet) was a popular summer resort for people in the Needles area. (Courtesy Dennis Casebier, Mojave Desert Archives, Goffs, California.)

NATIVE AMERICAN PETROGLYPHS. At a number of sites along the route, hikers might come upon relatively scarce images that people of the Mojave chipped into stone hundreds of years ago. These designs are believed to represent concern for natural resources and spiritual well-being. Archeologists are in the process of photographing and recording the petroglyphs in the California desert. Current studies of the patterns, placement, and location of rock art may reveal much concerning prehistoric life. The imperative for visiting these glyphs is "Do not disturb." These archeological resources are protected by the Federal Antiquities Act. (Courtesy Mojave River Valley Museum.)

20TH-CENTURY FOLK ART. A very different kind of stone recording can be observed along roadside berms between Essex and Cadiz Summit, which people along the road have termed "rock art." Names and dates and, occasionally, an ordeal of early Route 66 travel, are spelled out with rocks collected nearby. In the example above, the traveler simply wrote "Maddie." Others might have recorded the date of a broken axle or a flat tire. The writings serve as memorials to the ordeals of crossing the desert, and perhaps a sense that the travelers themselves were making history. (Courtesy Route 66 Corridor Preservation Program, National Park Service.)

ESSEX SHELL STATION. In 1931, U.S. Highway 66 was realigned on a more direct route west, and about six years later, students from Goffs were bussed to a school site along the road in Essex. Presumably on their way to or from school, students, the teacher, and other locals pose for a picture on a cool day. The bus looks more like an armored car than public transportation. But then, these were the days of Bonnie and Clyde, so perhaps safety was more important than a scenic trip. (Courtesy Dennis Casebier, Mojave Desert Archives, Goffs, California.)

DESERT STOPOVER IN CHAMBLESS. About halfway between Needles and Barstow, Chambless was a welcome way station in the trek across the Mojave before Interstate 40 provided a straighter route about 10 miles to the north. Little towns like Essex, Chambless, and Amboy depended on Route 66 travel. They were largely abandoned and left to decay when I-40 came and the Army scaled back. The two soldiers silhouetted near the gas pumps indicate that this picture would have been taken in the early 1940s. (Courtesy Mojave River Valley Museum.)

PATTON'S DESERT TRAINING CENTER. In preparation for the assault on Rommel's forces in North Africa, General Patton had his troops desert-seasoned in similar terrain and climate in the Mojave Desert around 1944. The training area was very close to America's Main Street near Chambless. Some said the heat was even worse here than in the Sahara. And odds are they all smoked Camels. (Courtesy Mojave River Valley Museum.)

ROADSIDE REST SPOT NEAR AMBOY. Shaded tables and benches along the road were placed to afford scenic views and picnic opportunities. They were maintained by the San Bernardino County Road Department. Now the responsibility has been assumed by the Bureau of Land Management (BLM). The BLM is also helping to install interpretive stations along the way. (Courtesy Vivian Davies.)

ROY'S OF AMBOY. The sign and adjacent facilities were welcome sights for tired and hungry motorists for over a half century. The facilities were operated from 1938 to 1999 by Buster Burris, "mayor" (owner) of Amboy. Almost to the millennium, Roy ran the only cafe and motel between Needles and Barstow that was still in first-class condition. Long a popular cafe and a destination stop for countless travelers, the building started out as a successful auto parts outlet. In 1945, Roy's Cafe took it over. It went downhill with the passing of Buster Burris, but a new owner has recently acquired the property, intending to restore and reestablish the motel and cafe business. (Courtesy Route 66 Corridor Preservation Program, National Park Service.)

Stopping for a Photograph near Amboy. With Amboy crater in the distance, this family group poses beside their homemade motor home in the 1930s. Think what an improvement the early Airstreams were over this mode of travel. (Courtesy Vivian Davies.)

Amboy Crater, 1930s. For Route 66ers who wonder about the two black mounds along the road, one just west of Amboy and the other a little west of Ludlow, listen up. They are volcanoes known as the Amboy and Pisgah craters. Geologists estimate that these volcanic twins probably erupted somewhere between 500 and 1,000 years ago, though not necessarily at the same time. In any event, they don't appear likely to do so again any time soon. In the 1950s, a bunch of Barstow High School students piled a load of old tires and other trash in the crater and set it afire; the thick black smoke had everyone thinking the volcano was coming alive, and the whole area was closed down for days until the hoax was discovered. Today the Bureau of Land Management maintains and protects the site. (Courtesy Mojave River Valley Museum.)

LEE YIM. A successful merchant poses with two young children in front of his ice cream shop. One interesting aspect of Ludlow history is revealed in the nearby cemetery. Tombstones dating back to the 1880s evidence a multiethnic community where people of many races and cultures are buried side by side. (Courtesy Mojave River Valley Museum.)

DESERT INN, HOTEL AND CAFE, LUDLOW, 1930s. In another shot taken at about the same time, we see the larger context of the little ice cream shop. The same two children appear to be playing in front of the hotel and cafe. According to writing on the snapshot, the pool hall next door had formerly been a cafe . . . and a barber shop. (Courtesy Mojave River Valley Museum.)

SHAMROCK CAFE AND GAS STATION. The Murphy brothers were the second owners of these roadside service facilities. In addition to gasoline and prepared food, the Murphys sold groceries and liquor. Interestingly, the property also included ruins of an abandoned 1908 Ludlow Mercantile Company building. The entire town is now owned by Knoll (family) Enterprises. (Courtesy Vivian Davies.)

LUDLOW CAFE AND UNION 76 STATION, 1947. The Moderne-style Ludlow Cafe of the 1940s continued to thrive into the 1950s and 1960s, owing to the town's location at an off-ramp of Interstate 40. The town still serves both Route 66 and interstate travelers. (Courtesy Vivian Davies, Virginia Knoll collection.)

DANGERS OF EARLY DESERT MOTORING. With no roads to follow and no direction signs, early motorists often became hopelessly lost and many perished in the heat. Later, when the Automobile Club of Southern California posted explicit warning signs—"Do not attempt this route without ample supplies of water, gas and oil"—there were always some who gambled and lost. This particular fellow, however, did not succumb to dehydration; the picture is of a crime scene east of Barstow. (Courtesy Mojave River Valley Museum.)

THEY DON'T MAKE THEM LIKE THIS ANYMORE. A late-1920s sedan is seen in topsy-turvy condition, with a broken rear axle and rear spare but otherwise almost intact. So who needed roll bars back then? This scene is reportedly on Route 66, mid-Mojave, and the picture appears to have been taken about 1930. (Courtesy Mojave River Valley Museum.)

THIS CAR DIDN'T FARE SO WELL. Apparently caught in a flash flood, this automobile was left to the sands of time. Travelers unfamiliar with the sudden and violent nature of these desert phenomena can easily find themselves in peril. Huge torrents of water may come from storms many miles away, threatening everything in their paths. This car may have been traveling a section of road alongside or crossing a stream bed and swept away by such a torrent. (Courtesy Mojave River Valley Museum.)

ROUTE 66ERS, 1930S. Somewhere along the way this unidentified family stopped to have their trip memorialized for posterity. Presumably they weren't driving one of the preceding vehicles. (Courtesy Mojave River Valley Museum.)

GENERAL STORE AND FILLING STATION, 1908. This Daggett landmark is still in operation, and the sign above the door tells us the store is over 100 years old, built before the National Old Trails road signs were posted. (Courtesy Mojave River Valley Museum.)

DAGGETT, 1940s. At one time, Daggett (formerly Calico Station) was the center of action in the Mojave. These three buildings—the Stone Hotel, pool hall, and grocery store—have long since ceased operation, but the town was once a "roaring camp" such as the one immortalized by writer Bret Harte. The hotel and pool hall were reportedly hangouts of "Death Valley Scotty." A narrow-gauge railroad hauled silver from Calico's Silver King mine, which was said to have yielded a total of $37 million worth of the metal during its years of production. Daggett also was the shipping center of a bustling borax mining industry. Nearby Mule Canyon hints of the fabled 20-mule teams that hauled the powdery mineral. (Courtesy Vivian Davies.)

DEATH VALLEY SCOTTY AND SHORTY HARRIS. Operating out of Daggett, where Scotty lived for many years, the two were undoubtedly the most famous (or infamous) of area prospectors. The Stone Hotel and pool hall were apparently two of Scotty's favorite haunts. (Courtesy Mojave River Valley Museum.)

SCOTTY'S CASTLE. Although he lived in and prospected out of Daggett, Death Valley Scotty is undoubtedly best known around the country for the resort hotel at Furnace Creek, in the middle of Death Valley. But it is not a castle and Scotty didn't build it. A wealthy Chicago mogul in poor health was more or less conned into investing in a non-existent gold mine by a "flamboyant prospector" (guess who). The investor and his wife did do alright though, by building a luxurious vacation home on the site. Always eager to grab the spotlight, Scotty then told reporters that it's "a shack I put up over my gold mine." The story spread and curiosity seekers from around the country flocked out to see him while the savvy Chicago businessman at last found a way to recoup his investment. (Courtesy Mojave River Valley Museum.)

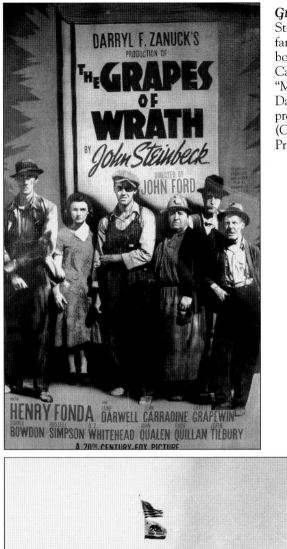

GRAPES OF WRATH MOVIE POSTER. John Steinbeck's classic book about migrant families struggling to recover from dust bowl deprivation and build a better life in California had already immortalized the "Mother Road" for millions of readers. Darryl Zanuck's 20th Century Fox production did the same for moviegoers. (Courtesy Route 66 Corridor Preservation Program, National Park Service.)

ORIGINAL DAGGETT INSPECTION STATION. Although the sign over the window reads "California Department of Agriculture," the station, built in 1930, was also manned by state police, charged with turning back migrants without money or jobs. The white sign at the left of the line of cars demands that all vehicles stop for inspection. (Courtesy Vivian Davies.)

The Joad Family wish you a Merry Christmas and hope to see you soon.

GRAPES OF WRATH CAST. This Christmas card was sent out to theater owners, studio executives, and the press. From left to right are Grandpa Joad (Charley Grapewin), Rosasharn (Dorris Bowden), Ma (Jane Darwell), Pa (Russell Simpson), Tom (Henry Fonda), Winfield (Darryl Hickman), Noah (Frank Sully), Ruthie (Shirley Mills), John (Frank Darien), Al (O. Z. Whitehead), Connie (Eddie Quillan), and Casy the preacher (John Carradine). This image captures some of the despair in the poignant scene in which the Joads are turned back by California's exclusionary policy of rejecting migrant workers who did not have $20 or evidence of a job waiting for them. The policy was enforced by state police at Route 66 "agricultural" inspection stations in Needles, Daggett (both on Route 66), and at Yermo. (Courtesy Victorville Route 66 Museum.)

NEW INSPECTION STATION. The station was enlarged in 1944 and operated until 1953. This photograph shows that the original building, at the rear, continued to be used. It has since been demolished. The newer one in front still stands as the only remaining migrant control station in the state. Although this was not the site actually used in the filming of *Grapes of Wrath*, (perhaps not sufficiently photogenic), the movie was a dramatic documentation of the activities actually carried out here. (Courtesy Vivian Davies.)

CALICO GHOST TOWN. Approximately five miles north of the road west of Daggett, sits what is left of the town of Calico. The essence of the historic town was captured in the Ghost Town Street at Knott's Berry Farm in Buena Park. The photograph is of the former drug store and bank in 1952. (Courtesy Mojave River Valley Museum.)

BARSTOW'S CALICO DAYS FESTIVAL. Held for many years in nearby Barstow, "Calico Days" was a solid tourist attraction. The event is now held in Calico and some of the bleak grittiness of its days as a desert mining town is gone. This "stagecoach" exhibit does seem, accurately, to suggest that silver mining was not the safest of occupations. (Courtesy Mojave River Valley Museum.)

Three

HIGH DESERT COMMUNITIES THROUGH THE MOUNTAINS

LINE OF TRAFFIC ENTERING BARSTOW, C. 1963. A Greyhound bus, presumably en route to L.A., ambles along in heavy afternoon traffic east of Barstow. These were the glory days of motoring on America's Main Street. Perhaps some of you, or your parents, were headed east or west along this stretch of road at about this time. (Courtesy Mojave River Valley Museum.)

ROSE INN. For decades, the Rose Inn, an attractive California Craftsman-style dining establishment in Barstow, welcomed motorists for home-cooked meals and charming ambience. It served breakfast, lunch, and dinner and was open until midnight. (Courtesy Mojave River Valley Museum.)

GILMORE GAS STATION. A classic 1950s service station was this Gilmore franchise on the road in Barstow. The Gilmores were a prominent Los Angeles family of the 20th century. A very similar Gilmore station still stands on Highland Avenue in Hollywood. In addition to the Gilmore Oil Company, there was a Gilmore Bank. The family founded and still owns the Farmers' Market on Fairfax in Los Angeles, which continues as a popular tourist destination and a favorite of Angelinos as well. CBS Television City now stands where a Gilmore baseball park once stood. (Courtesy Victorville Route 66 Museum.)

ATCHISON, TOPEKA & SANTA FE STREAMLINER. The then-futuristic model UP M1000 is on its maiden promotional trip in 1934, pulling into Barstow. On this historic event, the train arrives with one passenger (an overeager press agent) hanging out the side. In 1940, the train was reportedly scrapped for its aluminum. In the distance behind the train is a site that locals call "Placenta Hill." Supposedly, sometime in the past, for good luck, a woman had buried her newborn baby's umbilical cord and placenta on the hill. This was perhaps an urban legend, but the name stuck anyway, so perhaps the luck was good. (Courtesy Mojave River Valley Museum.)

SANTA FE RAIL STATION AND HARVEY HOUSE, BARSTOW. This shot, c. 1975, follows a tour group visiting the Italianate/Florentine Gothic train station, built in 1910. The station was the halfway point between Needles and Los Angeles and served as a major rest stop for rail as well as highway travelers. The early importance of the railroad to Barstow is evidenced by its naming, after William Barstow Strong, president of the Santa Fe Railroad. But Route 66 also played a very important role after motor travel became popular. Currently, the Barstow Route 66 Museum and Gift Shop share space in the building with a railroad museum and the local chamber of commerce. (Courtesy Mojave River Valley Museum.)

OASIS CAMP AUTO COURT AND TRAILER PARK. Neatly tucked behind a Flying "A" service station on Route 66, Oasis offered clean, modestly priced accommodations for weary motorists for several decades in the heydays of Route 66. (Courtesy Mojave River Valley Museum.)

ROUTE 66 AT NIGHT IN BARSTOW. This intersection with U.S. 91 and 466 was one of the busiest in the country in the 1950s. To illustrate the economic impact of the interstate, the Standard station at the lower right pumped about 800 gallons of gas per day the year before Route 40 bypassed downtown Barstow. After it was completed, that figure dropped to just 80 gallons a day. (Courtesy Mojave River Valley Museum.)

BEACON HOTEL, CAFE. Built in 1929 and 1930, by wealthy financiers undaunted by the stock market crash, the Spanish Colonial Revival Beacon Hotel, off to the left of this picture, was Barstow's finest. Hotel guests included F. Scott Fitzgerald, Norma Talmadge, and Mickey Rooney. It was demolished in 1970. The service station is still in operation thanks to support from Route 66 enthusiast Joe Mitchell. (Courtesy Mojave River Valley Museum.)

ROUTE 66 NEAR LENWOOD. A fairly barren stretch of road in the 1940s, this area is now part of Barstow. Here and there in this shot, one can spot vestiges of early roadside conveniences. A few still exist, though none are unaltered by time or human hand. Old Route 66 still parallels the Mojave River Basin, which can be identified by the line of cottonwood trees to the west, flanked by alfalfa fields. Cottonwood and alfalfa? Golly, Toto, we must be back in Kansas! (Courtesy Mojave River Valley Museum.)

ROADSIDE CONVENIENCE, HODGE. This service station, dating back to the National Old Trails era, continued to serve motorists well into Route 66 days. Hodge boasts the smallest federal building in the United States and, if anyone wants to play "smaller than thou" with the Hodgers, compare measurements on your own. (Courtesy Mojave River Valley Museum.)

PHOTO-OP AT THE HODGE GARAGE. At the tip of a hat, a new washer for the lady of the house! Are we looking at a Maytag salesman or a proud husband or son, *c.* 1934, with a surprise present? Whichever, it's the everyday life in the small towns along the road that we miss as we speed across today's sterile ribbons of concrete punctuated by look-alike, taste-alike, chain food dispensaries and pump-it-yourself gas stations. (Courtesy Mojave River Valley Museum.)

ROUTE 66 "WHOOP-DE-DO." Whenever possible, before the interstates, road building tended to follow the dips and curves of the natural landscapes. Modern technology has made driving a lot faster and perhaps safer, but the old feel of the land as we travel across the country is largely a thing of the past. (Courtesy Route 66 Corridor Preservation Program, National Park Service.)

SAGEBRUSH ANNIE'S. This is a great example of hand-crafted roadside vernacular architecture that dotted this popular section of the road near Helendale in pre-interstate days. The whole stretch of road between Victorville and Barstow has seen little development since the heyday of Route 66. With many gas stations, motels, and other roadside services now closed, some in ruins, it's a good place to do a little 20th-century "archeology" of road resources. Many maps of today don't even show Helendale. The nearby real estate development is called Silver Lakes. (Courtesy Route 66 Corridor Preservation Program, National Park Service.)

Victorville Garage (On Route 66 to the right of Bowers Drug Store)
Victorville, CA (Circa Early 1930s)

VICTORVILLE, 1920S. This is Bowers Rexall Drug Store along Route 66. First floor storefronts in the hotel also included a cleaning establishment. In the white building next to the drug store is a barbershop, back when barber poles were just about the only signage needed. On the far right is the Victorville Garage. (Courtesy Victorville Route 66 Museum.)

ROUTE THROUGH VICTORVILLE, 1940S. Late afternoon shadows hide shoppers' cars parked along the roadside. The street scene is looking east up Route 66 from the Stewart Hotel at the corner of Seventh Street. The sign on the right indicates mileage to Cajon Pass, San Bernardino, and Los Angeles. (Courtesy Security Pacific Collection, Los Angeles Public Library.)

38

RICHFIELD HI OCTANE. Although the photograph was taken about 1947, this Craftsman-style service station in Victorville probably dates back to the early 1920s. In any event, it's a very early predecessor of the Arco mini-mart/smog check stations. (Courtesy Victorville Route 66 Museum.)

VICTORVILLE ATTRACTIONS. This neon sign for the Green Spot Motel on Route 66 recalls the days when Victorville was the hot spot of the high desert, when Roy Rogers and Dale Evans reigned supreme. Victorville has a long history as a high desert resort community with scores of dude ranches and western-themed dining and "watering" holes. Undoubtedly the most famous resort was Roy and Dale's Apple Valley Inn. Victorville has since gradually become more of a bedroom community for people who work south of Cajon Pass, from San Bernardino on into Los Angeles. (Courtesy Route 66 Corridor Preservation Program, National Park Service.)

Mojave Travel, 1927. The exact location of this picture is unidentified, other than it was along Route 66. Most likely it was taken between Victorville and Cajon Pass. We do know that the date was 1927, the year after this stretch of road became Route 66. (Courtesy Vivian Davies.)

Vintage Fords on a Vintage Road. The early Ford V-8 Club of America, Mount Baldy Regional Group, and vintage car owners in Hesperia, are behind the wheels of their vehicles, enjoying a day out on a road as old as their automobiles. (Courtesy Vivian Davies.)

California or Bust! Like the covered wagons of the 19th-century pioneer families, this relic is laden with whatever the migrant household could carry and would survive the trip. If on the road at the time this photograph was taken, the travelers are in the wrong place to get gasoline though! (Courtesy Victorville Route 66 Museum.)

41

1940s Greyhound Bus Stop at Meekers. Travelers stretch, snap photographs, and enjoy refreshments at Meekers Cafe in Cajon Pass. The cafe and garage were welcome roadside amenities for several decades. The garage, however, predated the arroyo stone restaurant by several years. Note the "fenders" painted on the Greyhound bus. (Courtesy Victorville Route 66 Museum.)

Antique Car Rally at the Summit Inn. Still in operation today, the Summit Inn in Phelan has a long history on the road and is one of the most popular places to eat. Here a passel of antique car buffs stop to recharge their energies and chat with fellow travelers. Cajon Pass and Camp Cajon were strategically important command posts for Spanish and Mormon settlers. The first paved road was established in the 1920s, but the floods of 1938 wiped out large sections of the road, as well as Camp Cajon, which had become a popular tourist attraction. (Courtesy Victorville Route 66 Museum.)

INTERIOR, SUMMIT INN. This is what the car buffs in the preceding photograph came for. The Summit Inn has had a place in road lore for a long time and will likely continue to please palates well into the future. (Courtesy Route 66 Corridor Preservation Program, National Park Service.)

CAJON PASS ROAD IMPROVEMENTS. A new alignment of the road through Cajon Pass is recorded on this 1939 bridge. The crease that runs parallel, just past the telephone lines beyond the bridge, may be an earlier alignment of Route 66. There are at least five old alignments of the road through Cajon Pass, but only a fairly short seven-mile segment of one is drivable. Once one of the very early divided highways, it runs between Cleghorn and Kenwood. (Courtesy Route 66 Corridor Preservation Program, National Park Service.)

Four

FOOTHILL COMMUNITIES

SAN BERNARDINO MOUNTAINS AND ORANGE GROVES. One of the most impressive features of early travel across the San Gabriel Valley on Route 66 from San Bernardino down to the Arroyo Seco in South Pasadena were mile upon mile of citrus groves, framed by snowcapped mountains. The aroma at blossom time was as intoxicating as the scenery was breathtaking. (Courtesy Security Pacific Collection, Los Angeles Public Library.)

1928 NATIONAL ORANGE SHOW IN SAN BERNARDINO. A young woman poses with a crate of oranges. Orange festivals still continue to attract visitors in nearby Riverside, but agricultural acreage continues to shrink from urban sprawl and industrial development. (Courtesy Security Pacific Collection, Los Angeles Public Library)

CALIFORNIA THEATER, C. 1935. The Spanish-Moorish California Theater on Highland Avenue was the premiere theater in the vast San Bernardino County. The California no longer shows movies, but plays and musical events are still staged here. This is where Will Rogers made his last public appearance before he and aviation legend Wiley Post were killed in a plane crash near Point Barrow, Alaska, in August 1935. (Courtesy Security Pacific Collection, Los Angeles Public Library.)

1920s Road Sign to Tourist Diversions. The Southern California Auto Club was never far away, always eager to tell us where to go. (Courtesy Goodspeed Corpe and Pat Krig.)

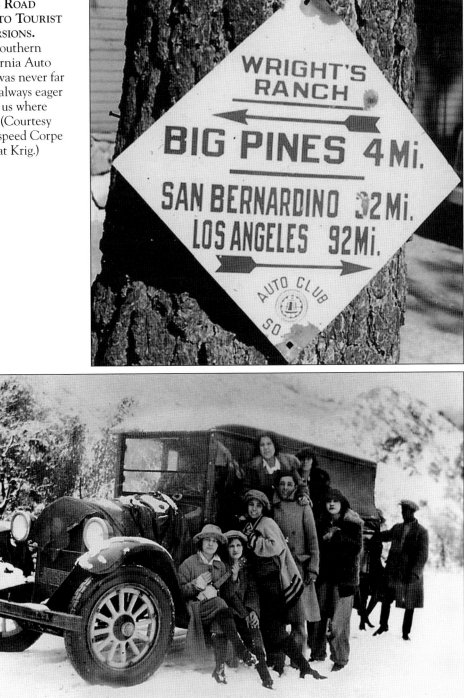

A Side Trip to Wrightwood. Julia and Eloise Arciniega are depicted with friends on an outing to the snow, north of Route 66 near San Bernardino. Their vehicle appears like it could stand in as a late 1920s model for the currently ubiquitous "Soccer Mom" SUV of today. (Courtesy Shades of L.A. Archives, Los Angeles Public Library.)

ORIGINAL MCDONALD'S. Focusing on lower prices, high volume, and speedy service, Richard and Maurice McDonald opened this "speedee service—buy 'em by the bag" restaurant on December 12, 1948. They had previously run a successful barbeque restaurant in San Bernardino. In 1961, the McDonalds sold the business and name to Ray Kroc, who pioneered the fast food franchise system and made McDonald's one of the most successful food enterprises in the world. How fortunate he did not change the name; customers might have been reluctant to "buy 'em by the Kroc." (Courtesy Nick Cataldo and McDonald's Museum.)

Mount Vernon Avenue, c. 1963. After coming down the mountains, this is the primary Route 66 path through central San Bernardino, before the route heads west toward Pasadena. Mitla Cafe, a popular spot for home-style Mexican food, is on the left side of the street. Many 66ers will be pleased to hear that Mitla is still in business and as good as ever. (Courtesy San Bernardino Library.)

Route 66 Directions to McDonald's Site. This sign in San Bernardino invites a trip back into fast-food history. It's only a few blocks off the route, but don't expect to find the original building or prices. (Courtesy Route 66 Corridor Preservation Program, National Park Service.)

Route 66 Rendezvous. Back in the heyday of the "Mother Road," San Bernardino was a Route 66 town. And for over a decade, the city has kept the old 1930s to 1960s nostalgia alive with the annual Route 66 Rendezvous. For four days in September, over 2,000 classic cars cruise and then park along downtown streets. An estimated crowd of 250,000 attended on September 18, 2000, when this photograph was taken. (Courtesy Nick Cataldo and *The San Bernardino Sun* newspaper)

HIGH-LEVEL ROUTE 66 "RENDEZVIEWERS." San Bernardino Mayor Judith Valles, left, state senator Nell Soto, and Stater Brothers president and CEO Jack Brown are having a great time at the 2000 Route 66 Rendezvous. With many of their supermarkets along the route in San Bernardino County, the company has enthusiastically sponsored and supported the rendezvous for several years. (Courtesy Nick Cataldo and *The San Bernardino Sun* newspaper.)

WIGWAM MOTEL. The motel opened in 1950 with 11 tepees, then added eight more in 1954. The "Do it in a Tee Pee" sign and well-maintained accommodations seem to keep the tepees fairly teeming with travelers almost year-round. It's served by the Rialto post office, but is actually in the City of San Bernardino. (Courtesy Route 66 Corridor Preservation Program, National Park Service.)

ORANGE JUICE STAND AND BONO'S ITALIAN RESTAURANT. This surviving orange juice stand is only one of many dozen that dotted Route 66 along the orange groves in the 1920s and 1930s. Many restaurants of today in this former citrus growing region started out as orange juice stands. As food was added to command more tourist dollars, the evolution gained momentum. This last of the old juice stands was moved to this location in 1993 next to Bono's to be spared from the wrecking ball. Bono's is itself a treasured Mother Road heritage resource, having faithfully served travelers since 1936. (Courtesy Route 66 Corridor Preservation Program, National Park Service.)

A ROUTE 66 HONEYMOON. Charles McLaughlin and his bride are preparing here to leave on their honeymoon to the Grand Canyon on September 12, 1927, just a year after U.S. Highway 66 was established. They would take Route 66 most of the way in his 1925 Chevrolet. (Courtesy John Anthony Adams.)

FRANCIS "FANNY" POWELL'S RIALTO SERVICE STATION, C. 1938. Here in the Foothill Boulevard station, attendants (including a future Rialto city planning director) come out to check customers's tires and water, pump the gas, wash windshields, and, above all, seemingly enjoy the work. One customer recalled Fanny Powell as being blue-eyed, very handsome, and with a huge smile. The station was a favorite hangout for the local men. (Courtesy John Anthony Adams.)

ORANGE BAR, RIALTO. How could you pass this place without your mouth beginning to water? This 1940s fruit stand at the northeast corner of Foothill and Eucalyptus, was in operation until the 1950s. All the cold, fresh-squeezed orange juice a customer could drink could be had for only 15¢. The last proprietor said Spencer Tracy once stopped for a glass. (Courtesy John Anthony Adams.)

FONTANA INTERSECTION, 1929. Looking East on Foothill at Sierra Fontana, and taken shortly after Route 66 first came by here, this photograph shows a nice new road lined with palm trees through prosperous orchards. (Courtesy John Anicic.)

FONTANA INTERSECTION, 1944. The same view of the same area as above shows 15 years of age, meaning curbs, roadside stands, and signage indicative of the first approach of exurbia. (Courtesy John Anicic.)

FONTANA INTERSECTION, 1950S. Only a decade later, postwar development has transformed the same intersection from an agricultural landscape into a bustling thoroughfare. This is the heyday of Route 66, when entrepreneurs of every stripe sought to fill the need for roadside services. (Courtesy John Anicic.)

FONTANA INTERSECTION, 2005. This is what the intersection looks like today. The street has been substantially widened and the Foothill corridor "suburbanized" by moving the commercial establishments back off of the streets into shopping plazas. Roadside services are harder to spot. (Courtesy Glen Duncan, California Route 66 Preservation Foundation)

RANCHO CUCAMONGA, 1959. A classic postcard shot depicts a spot a little further west along the former agricultural paradise between San Bernardino and Los Angeles. This shot looks East on Foothill from Archibald. We don't have an earlier view of this area, when it was covered in vineyards, but the transformation here paralleled what occurred in Rialto, Fontana, and across the San Gabriel Valley. (Courtesy John Anicic.)

ENDANGERED 1920S GAS STATION. This pristine Standard Station in Rancho Cucamonga is threatened by development unless planners and developers have the vision and ability to integrate the historic structures into their plans. The right side (eastern end) of the garage structure was demolished many years ago for a couple of characterless storefronts (Courtesy Vivian Davies.)

MADONNA OF THE TRAIL. This memorial statue on Euclid Avenue facing Foothill Boulevard in Upland was placed by the National Society of the Daughters of the American Revolution. It is dedicated to the pioneer mothers of the covered wagon days. Long before it became part of Route 66, Foothill Boulevard followed the course of the National Old Trails Road, which, as its name implies, was an improved version of an old wagon trail. Then, too, the pioneer settlers had followed footpaths of the old Mojave Trail. The Madonna of the Trail overlooks a broad, park-like promenade lined with pepper and acacia trees that accent Euclid between the San Gabriel foothills down through Upland's charming historic community. (Courtesy Route 66 Corridor Preservation Program, National Park Service.)

CITRUS PROCESSING, 1930. Although the sign in this facility clearly reads "Upland Citrus Association," the fruit in the foreground bin looks more like apples. But in black and white, who can tell? In addition to oranges and lemons, area orchards also produced apples, almonds, and a variety of agricultural products. (Courtesy Security Pacific Collection, Los Angeles Public Library.)

OLD SCHOOL HOUSE, CLAREMONT. Now a mixed-use facility with a large area available for special events, the building was originally the Claremont High School Gymnasium. The site has also been home to Griswold's Inn and Restaurant, a popular Smorgasbord and Candlelight Theater venue known throughout the region. (Courtesy Glen Duncan, California Route 66 Preservation Foundation.)

ROUTE 66 CORRIDOR CULTURAL LANDSCAPE. Built in 1931, with a grassy median lined with eucalyptus trees, this four-lane parkway in Claremont is one of the most beautiful historic sections of the route in California that still exist. (Courtesy Glen Duncan, California Route 66 Preservation Foundation)

TUGBOAT ANNIE'S. Built in the late 1960s, this one-of-kind example of "Fantasyland" architecture is no longer operated as Tugboat Annie's, and has recently gone through several changes in management. As of this writing, its latest iteration is as a sushi restaurant. That still conveys the message of fresh fish, although in landlocked Claremont, this tugboat is moored in a sea of asphalt. (Courtesy Glen Duncan, California Route 66 Preservation Foundation.)

COATES BICYCLES. A fine example of Route 66 neon of the 1950s and 1960s, this sign on Foothill is still in near mint condition. The bicycle shop moved here from an early location in downtown Pomona. (Courtesy Glen Duncan, California Route 66 Preservation Foundation.)

HENRY'S DRIVE-IN, POMONA. One of the most beautiful and architecturally significant ultramodern drive-in restaurants ever built, John Lautner's classic Henry's on Foothill Boulevard was completed in 1957. The design artfully integrated interior and exterior spaces, but was demolished several years ago after serving for a time as a discotheque. According to architect Alan Hess, Route 66 travelers who came here after crossing the parched Mojave found this a "cool, shaded oasis under a broad oval roof carried by a deep laminated wood spine. Henry's combined a drive-in, coffee shop, and restaurant." (Courtesy Alan Hess; photograph by Julius Schulman.)

LA VERNE'S LA PALOMA. A prominent Mexican restaurant with great curb appeal on Foothill Boulevard, La Paloma may be remembered by Route 66ers in its former iteration as Wilson's Restaurant, which was a local favorite for many years. (Courtesy Glen Duncan, California Route 66 Preservation Foundation)

WALT WILEY'S DRIVE-IN. This Craftsman-influenced Four Square restaurant at Grand Avenue and Alosta in Glendora was a great hangout for young people in the 1940s. It survived until 2002 as the Hickory Inn, but, alas, the site was sacrificed to one of the great bulldozers of history, Walgreen's. Glendora otherwise qualifies as a die-hard Route 66 destination. (Courtesy John David Landers and the Glendora Historical Society.)

PALM TROPICS, GLENDORA.
This roadside convenience, with its backdrop of the San Gabriel Mountains, is one of many attractive motels along the route through Glendora, which also sports many surviving trailer parks. The community may have the most Route 66 signs per mile of any city in the eight-state corridor. They are almost everywhere along Alosta, except perhaps the classy 80-plus-year-old Golden Spur Restaurant, featured in the neon display on page 63. The Golden Spur, incidentally, was originally a hamburger stand on a dirt road, with a hitching rack out front for local cowboys to secure their horses. (Courtesy Glen Duncan, California Route 66 Preservation Foundation)

"Neon Highway" in California. Here's a sample of well-preserved or restored neon signage across Route 66 in San Bernardino and Los Angeles Counties. Pictured are (above left) the Magic Lamp Inn in Rancho Cucamonga, (below left) the Sycamore Inn in Rancho Cucamonga, (above right) The Golden Spur in Glendora, and (below right) Whistle Stop Trains in Pasadena. (Courtesy Glen Duncan, California Route 66 Preservation Foundation.)

AZUSA DRIVE-IN. As ubiquitous as drive-in theaters were in the 1950s and 1960s, very few have survived the gobbling up by suburban sprawl. This one is no longer operated as a venue for watching movies from the semi-privacy of your car. However, the essential historic integrity of the marquee, screen, and "parking" area is intact. In fact, the large expanse facing the screen is a parking lot for Azusa Pacific University. One might hope university planners might see the benefit of continued preservation and perhaps combining this use with double-duty service as an outdoor presentation arena. (Courtesy Glen Duncan, California Route 66 Preservation Foundation.)

HONEYVILLE. This roadside restaurant and apiary at Foothill and La Loma in Duarte satisfied a lot of tourists' sweet teeth, and the bees were a boon to local orchards. (Courtesy Duarte Historical Society.)

TRAILS RESTAURANT IN DUARTE. Recently demolished to make way for a residential development, the Trails was a beloved roadside attraction with many devoted fans and patrons. Unfortunately, none had any "juice" with Duarte movers and shakers, so the sign was moved and the restaurant was shaken down. (Courtesy Route 66 Corridor Preservation Program, National Park Service.)

DUARTE LILY. Like its neighbors, Duarte was prime citrus orchard land in the days of the National Old Trails Roads and early Route 66 days. This is one of the many orange crate labels archived at the excellent local museum. (Courtesy Duarte Historical Society.)

WHITE OAK AVENUE (NOW FOOTHILL BOULEVARD). Lined with pepper trees planted by "Lucky" Baldwin, this picturesque section of the Route 66 corridor in Monrovia was a favorite route of movie people from Hollywood to Palm Springs in the late 1920s and early 1930s. The trees were cut down in 1931, when the street was widened. Oh, for a two-lane blacktop this free of traffic anywhere in Los Angeles County in this day and age! (Courtesy Security Pacific Collection, Los Angeles Public Library.)

MONROVIA FILLING STATION. Still up and standing, but not in business, this old gas station on Shamrock Avenue on the route up from Huntington Drive to Foothill has been used in several films to authenticate roadside stations of the 1920s, 1930s, and 1940s. An adjacent airport and an early drive-in restaurant that predated McDonald's are both gone. (Courtesy Glen Duncan, California Route 66 Preservation Foundation.)

AZTEC HOTEL, MONROVIA. Designed by prominent architect Robert Stacy Judd for a group of Monrovia investors in 1925, the Aztec was actually inspired by Mayan architecture. Mr. Judd, however, felt the term "Aztec" was more exotic and better known. The hotel was an immediate sensation and the bar a popular stopover for Hollywood celebrities on the way to Palm Springs. The hotel has been listed on the National Register of Historic Places since 1977. The Aztec is now undergoing restoration and renovation and should one day take its rightful place as one of the most outstanding tourist destinations on Route 66. (Courtesy Security Pacific Collection, Los Angeles Public Library.)

AZTEC HOTEL NEON SIGN RESTORED. As a first step in a major restoration, the 1925 neon hotel sign once again welcomes visitors to a rip-roaring good time in the Brass Elephant Bar and a sparkling array of entertainment events held at the Mayan-inspired hotel. (Courtesy Glen Duncan, California Route 66 Preservation Foundation.)

SANTA ANITA INTERNMENT CAMP. Beginning April 3, 1942, in the same parking lot which once held seas of limousines, jalopies, and family sedans of horseracing fans, a miniature city of frame houses and barracks was built to house 3,200 Japanese Americans who were forced from their homes by U.S. policy during World War II. In the foreground is the track's saddling paddock where the horses paraded just before their races. (Courtesy *Herald-Examiner* Collection, Los Angeles Public Library.)

AMERICA'S RACEHORSE ALONG AMERICA'S MAIN STREET. Seabiscuit, on the outside, and Kayak II stretch their legs in a workout on January 29, 1940, between races for the public over the weekend at Santa Anita Racetrack. Although neither horse was pushed, Kayak II's performance captured public fancy. Yet by the end of February when the two horses met in the sixth running of the $100,000 Santa Anita Handicap, the 'Biscuit was expected to go to post a six-to-five favorite. Do you know who won? (Courtesy *Herald-Examiner* Collection Sports Exhibit, Los Angeles Public Library.)

Five

ARROYO SECO COMMUNITIES

RENOWN HOTEL'S EARTHQUAKE DAMAGE. On March 10, 1933, the Huntington Hotel, on Oak Knoll in Pasadena, approximately a mile south of Route 66, was hit hard by seismic activity. The Huntington had long been a favorite of well-heeled tourists and was always packed at Rose Bowl time in Route 66 days, when the road brought thousands of football and parade fans from the east and Midwest. Rebuilt shortly afterward and remodeled again in the current era, The Huntington is now operated by the Ritz-Carlton organization. (Courtesy Shades of L.A. Archives, Los Angeles Public Library.)

SAGA MOTOR HOTEL, COLORADO BOULEVARD, PASADENA. At least to one dedicated Route 66er who has traveled the full length of the road many times, this quintessential California motel from the 1950s ranks as one of the top places to stay anywhere along the route. (Courtesy Glen Duncan, California Route 66 Preservation Foundation.)

CHURRIGUERESQUE PACKARD SHOWROOM, 1920S. No longer peddling Packards, this showroom is nonetheless a true icon of the Roaring Twenties fascination with the automobile in Southern California. At that time, per capita car ownership in Pasadena was the highest in the country. (Courtesy Glen Duncan, California Route 66 Preservation Foundation)

MOTHER GOOSE PANTRY. Situated along Colorado Boulevard in 1925, a year before Route 66 was officially born, the enterprising people who ran this restaurant were soon to be visited by "so many tourists they wouldn't know what to do!" An early example of "programmatic architecture," the Mother Goose Pantry has not survived. (Courtesy Security Pacific Collection, Los Angeles Public Library.)

EINSTEIN AT CAL TECH, C. 1930. Just four blocks south of the Route 66 Colorado Boulevard alignment, the California Institute of Technology had become one of the premiere scientific institutions in the country, drawing such notables as Albert Einstein, Robert Millikan, and Albert Michelson to study and teach here. This photograph shows Dr. Einstein stepping into an automobile, probably not on his way to the Mother Goose Pantry. (Courtesy Security Pacific Collection, Los Angeles Public Library.)

WAITING TO SMELL THE ROSES. On Colorado Boulevard, just prior to dawn on January 1, 1963, eager spectators line Route 66 in Pasadena, waiting for the Tournament of Roses Parade. With USC and Wisconsin playing in the Rose Bowl later in the day, a goodly number of these spectators most likely drove out on the full length of "America's Main Street" to watch the parade up close and cheer on the Wisconsin Badgers. (Courtesy Pasadena Museum of History Archives.)

JACKIE ROBINSON, PASADENA JUNIOR COLLEGE, 1939. Long before he broke Major League Baseball's color line with the Brooklyn Dodgers, Jackie Robinson starred at Pasadena's Muir High School, at Pasadena Junior College, and then at UCLA. During the 1940s, Jackie also played professionally with the L.A. Bulldogs (football) and the L.A. Red Devils (basketball). According to eyewitnesses, the 5-foot-10 Robinson was one of the first players to dunk a basketball. After his success in the majors, he portrayed himself in the film *The Jackie Robinson Story* with Ruby Dee. (Courtesy *Herald-Examiner* Collection Sports Exhibit, Los Angeles Public Library.)

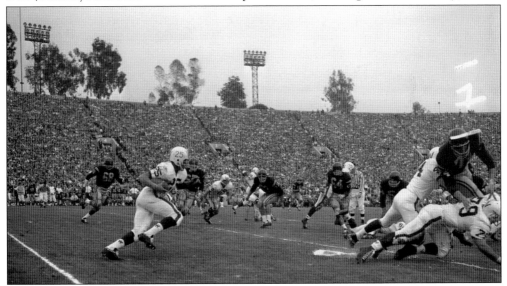

1963 ROSE BOWL, PASADENA—A ROUTE 66 EVENT. The game, between the University of Wisconsin Badgers and the University of Southern California Trojans, pitted teams from both ends of the road in the conflict. Big Ten and Wisconsin fans who drove 2,200 or more miles to get here had to settle for good weather or possibly a trip to Disneyland or a drive down Sunset strip. USC won, 42-37. (Courtesy Pasadena Museum of History Archives.)

RALPHS GROCERY, 1929. This stylish building on Lake Avenue, just north of Colorado, by architects Morgan, Walls, and Clements has (sadly) long since been demolished. It is quite similar to and was built by the same team that designed Chapman Market on Sixth in Los Angeles, which has been nicely restored. (Courtesy Security Pacific Collection, Los Angeles Public Library.)

TRAIN CROSSING COLORADO BOULEVARD. Route 66 and the Santa Fe Railroad cross paths many times across California. However, this intersection, c. 1938, near the old Tower Theater just east of Fair Oaks, is surely one of the more dramatic, being at grade across a busy thoroughfare. Gold Line commuter trains now use the old Santa Fe right-of-way, but are underground at this point. (Courtesy Security Pacific Collection, Los Angeles Public Library.)

COLORADO BOULEVARD, 1950s. Unlike the nifty Mercury and the Chevy station wagon, which might possibly have been restored and still be in operation, Pasadena's Nash's Department Store is a thing of the storied past. Even as altered here with awnings and display windows that debase the stylish art deco facade, it would have been nice if Nash's could have rambled on into the present day. Note two other 1950s relics at the right of Nash's: an Arthur Murray dance studio and an S&H Green Stamps showroom. (Courtesy Pasadena Museum of History Archives.)

STREAMLINE MODERNE SKATING RINK. This building is now a public storage facility, but at least the exterior is relatively intact. The Winter Gardens skating rink, designed by architect Cyril Bennett, was built the same year the Mother Road was realigned to join with the new Arroyo Seco Parkway in 1940. Bennett also designed the Pasadena Civic Auditorium and Masonic Temple. Winter Gardens closed in 1966 and for a time the building was a post office annex. (Courtesy California Route 66 Preservation Foundation.)

PASADENA'S HOTEL GREEN. Frederick Roehrig built this landmark hotel in two stages, the first, in 1898, included an enclosed bridge crossing Raymond Avenue, seen heading southward to the left. The portion on the east side of Raymond was almost totally demolished in the 1930s. The portion here on the left, expanded in 1903, now houses the Castle Green Apartments. This photograph was apparently taken in between the two phases of construction. The elegant walkways are gone, but a park, of sorts, still serves for periodic craft fairs and concerts. Fair Oaks Avenue, the wide thoroughfare on the right, leads down through South Pasadena. The historic Raymond Hotel (second iteration) can be seen atop Raymond Hill in the distance. (Courtesy Seaver Center for Western History Research, Natural History Museum of Los Angeles County.)

RAYMOND HOTEL, SOUTH PASADENA, C. 1920. The first Raymond Hotel, a huge Second Empire-style structure, was built in 1886, but burned to the ground on Easter Sunday, 1895. This attractive Mission Revival replacement was opened in December 1901 and survived until the middle of the Great Depression. Like the Hotel Green, in its big sister city to the north, the Raymond predated Route 66 by many years. These hotels along the most serviceable route into Los Angeles were undoubtedly part of the reason transportation planners selected this route in the first place. They probably were unaware, however, that immediately adjacent to the Raymond Hotel is an adobe where the Mexican high command met in January 1847 and decided to capitulate to American forces under Colonel Fremont. A mere stone's throw away from where Route 66 passes through South Pasadena is thus where the decision to end the Mexican Colonial period in California was made. (Courtesy Seaver Center for Western History Research, Natural History Museum of Los Angeles County.)

RAYMOND STATION. This Santa Fe Railway stop is another memorial to the parallel courses of the railroad and U.S. Highway 66. Here on Fair Oaks Avenue is the old depot that served the elegant Raymond Hotel resort. The hotel was shuttered in 1934, but the charming station was not demolished until 1961, a few years after this shot was taken. (Courtesy South Pasadena Preservation Foundation.)

RAYMOND PHARMACY. This 1933 photograph of the pharmacy at Fair Oaks Avenue and Mission Street shows the building with the white glazed brick cladding unaltered, as built in 1913 by architect Arthur Benton (who had recently worked on the Mission Inn in Riverside). The property owner-developer was Mrs. Gertrude Ozmun, who owned a number of properties in South Pasadena and Southern California including the former home of Madame Modjeska in Tustin. (Courtesy Meredith and Michael Miller Collection.)

FAIR OAKS PHARMACY, SOUTH PASADENA. Although the property has changed hands several times and surfaces altered, the corner unit has been continuously operated as a pharmacy since 1913. The original soda fountain had been removed in an earlier remodel. But wishing to restore that feature, recent business owners purchased a soda fountain and drug store cabinetry that had been in previous use at another Route 66 pharmacy in Joplin, Missouri. The author recalls going to that pharmacy as a young boy while visiting grandparents nearby in the Baxter Springs, Kansas, area. (Courtesy California Route 66 Preservation Foundation.)

SOUTH PASADENA CITY HALL. The two story Classical Revival city hall, police station, jail, and fire station, which stood guard over the Mission Street alignment from the early to mid-1930s, was designed by Norman Foote Marsh in 1914. In 1949, the city stripped the building of its architectural adornment for a more modern look. In the late 1980s, the building, lacking any historic character, was demolished. (Courtesy South Pasadena Preservation Foundation.)

RIALTO THEATER. Built in 1925 by theater architect L. A. Smith, the Spanish Baroque/Moorish/Eclectic-style Rialto was the premiere theater for the entire San Gabriel Valley. It featured a theater organ to accompany silent films, and the movies were preceded by vaudeville acts on weekends. The Rialto badly needs rehabilitation. If the current plans of the local Downtown Redevelopment Commission hold true, the theater may have a bright future indeed. (Courtesy Route 66 Corridor Preservation Program, National Park Service.)

FORMER EL CENTRO DRIVE-IN MARKET. Drive-in markets were the first non-automotive retail form to accommodate customers arriving by car. Almost all were built in car-crazy Southern California between 1926 and 1934. This one on the 1931–1935 Route 66 alignment on Mission Street in South Pasadena was saved from demolition by the declaration of its eligibility for a National Register listing. Instead, it was given sensitive adaptive re-use rehabilitation. Significant architectural features and the feeling of open grocery bays were preserved and the automotive forecourt became a pedestrian-friendly pocket park. (Courtesy Glen Duncan, California Route 66 Preservation Foundation.)

COLORADO STREET BRIDGE AND VISTA DEL ARROYO. This graceful bridge, completed in 1913, became part of Route 66 from about 1936 to 1940, the only time in which the route did not go through South Pasadena. It is a marvel in design and engineering by John Alexander Low Waddell, of Waddell and Harrington of Kansas City. Waddell and Harrington were American pioneers in reinforced concrete (the Greene brothers brought in an Italian engineer for their 1906 Oaklawn Bridge along Route 66, two miles south). Painstaking restoration of the Colorado Street Bridge was completed in 1993 and Pasadena Heritage has hosted a festive "Bridge Party" every year in June on and around the historic span. The former Vista Del Arroyo Hotel, seen here on the east bank of the Arroyo Seco, was built in 1920 by Marston and Van Pelt. The distinctive tower was added 10 years later by George Wiemeyer. The building now houses the Ninth Circuit Court of Appeals and the Western Justice Center. (Courtesy Seaver Center for Western History Research, Natural History Museum of Los Angeles County.)

CAWSTON OSTRICH FARM. Operated from the 1890s through 1934, the ostrich farm in South Pasadena was one of the most popular Southern California tourist attractions of the early 20th century. Not only were the feathers in great demand for adorning women's hats, fans, and whatever, but riding astride one of the big birds or being pulled along in an ostrich carriage served as a turn-of-the-century theme-park ride. This photograph of African American tourists was taken in 1927. (Courtesy Shades of L.A. Archives, Los Angeles Public Library.)

BEAUTY OF THE ARROYO SECO. Extending from foothills in the San Gabriel Mountains north of Altadena, past Brookside Golf Course, the Rose Bowl, Colorado Street Bridge, soccer fields, and baseball diamonds in South Pasadena, Sycamore Grove Park in Highland Park, and the River Center at its confluence with the Los Angeles River, the Arroyo Seco is one of Southern California's greatest natural wonders. It has inspired successive generations of artists and stimulated an "arroyo culture" that persists today. This picture of Busch Gardens in Pasadena captures a page from the past in the arroyo heritage. Built in the early 20th century, the gardens have long since been virtually swallowed up by urban sprawl. This spot would have been about a mile north of the place where Route 66 joined with the Arroyo in its last alignment down into Los Angeles. (Courtesy Pasadena Museum of History Archives.)

A FOGGY DAY AT THE YORK STREET BRIDGE, C. 1931. Built in 1911 and jointly financed by the City of South Pasadena and the County of Los Angeles (with an added contribution from Walter Cawston for decorative adornments), the York Street Bridge across the Arroyo Seco was destined to become part of one Route 66 alignment and an accoutrement of another. The transitional alignment crossed the bridge from 1931 to 1935. Then in 1940, when the parkway was completed, Route 66 ran underneath. (Courtesy Pasadena Museum of History Archives.)

A SOUTHERN CALIFORNIA CHRISTMAS IN THE GREAT DEPRESSION. H. B. Ware and his family may have been evicted from Terminal Island, where they have been camping out due to Depression-era circumstances. Whether the family came as recent migrants from the dust bowl or had previously lived in some part of the Los Angeles area is not known. Times were hard for most people in the 1930s. (Courtesy *Herald-Examiner* Collection, Los Angeles Public Library.)

FEED RACK, EAGLE ROCK. Originally built as an ice cream parlor on Colorado Boulevard, a few blocks west of Eagle Rock Boulevard, where Route 66 turned south, this small building became a restaurant during the Depression. Even with oversized ice cream cones at each corner, the restaurant typifies Depression-era marketing along the road: "Hello Old Timer! Are You Broke and Hungry? Stop and get some Coffee and Donuts. They are on us." (Courtesy Security Pacific Collection, Los Angeles Public Library.)

LOS ANGELES POLICE MUSEUM. On York Street, only a couple of blocks west of Figueroa, which was part of Route 66 for most of the 1930s, the former Highland Park police station is now a "must-see" museum of L.A. crime and crime fighting. Vintage police cars, and several bullet-riddled vehicles used in infamous Los Angeles criminal pursuits, are on display. (Courtesy Security Pacific Collection, Los Angeles Public Library)

SOUTHWEST MUSEUM AND CASA DE ADOBE. Now operated by the Autry National Center, these two facilities are individual treasures, each in their own right. The Southwest Museum has the second largest collection of Native American artifacts in the world, bested only by the Smithsonian. The Casa de Adobe was built in 1925 to depict a typical Mexican Colonial era ranchero. It is a square adobe hacienda with a single tier of rooms, including a chapel, all facing a central courtyard. (Courtesy Security Pacific Collection, Los Angeles Public Library.)

EL ALISAL, C. 1960. Charles Fletcher Lummis was a folklorist, photographer, author, archeologist, archivist, and ethnographer, who founded the Southwest Museum and saved four old Missions. His former home, El Alisal, is now the headquarters of the Historical Society of Southern California. Lummis was an early and indefatigable promoter of the Arroyo Seco artists community. As such, he helped define the character of cities and communities that grew up along the arroyo. (Courtesy *Herald-Examiner* Collection, Los Angeles Public Library.)

IOWA STATE PICNIC AT SYCAMORE GROVE PARK, C. 1928. In the early days of exuberant Route 66 travel, well-organized state tour groups from all across the country would descend upon Southern California to reunite with their transplanted alumni and savor the sunny, subtropical paradise. Beautiful Sycamore Grove Park of the 1920s and 1930s played host to dozens of state picnics. This group is from Iowa, but New Yorkers and Pennsylvanians, too, were drawn to this charming retreat in the Arroyo Seco. (Courtesy Security Pacific Collection, Los Angeles Public Library.)

ARROYO SECO PARKWAY OPENING. Rose Queen Sally Stanton, Gov. Culbert L. Olsen, and other dignitaries attend the 1940 dedication. Designed for a maximum speed of 45 miles per hour, the parkway was a huge step in Southern California transportation, giving Route 66 a nonstop throughway from Pasadena to downtown Los Angeles, free of traffic lights and stop signs. (Courtesy *Herald-Examiner* Collection, Los Angeles Public Library.)

ARROYO SECO PARKWAY, WHEN IT LOOKED LIKE A PARKWAY. Now virtually indistinguishable from freeways that abound in Southern California, the Arroyo Seco was a true parkway when designated as part of Route 66 in 1940. As a parkway, it was designed for maximum speeds of 40 miles per hour to make urban motoring a pleasant, leisurely experience. This photograph was taken from underneath the York Street Bridge, shown in a previous picture. Current "Pasadena Freeway" postings of 55 and 60 miles per hour are largely ignored, even though the Arroyo's meandering path restricts visibility; the safety of even these posted speeds is questionable. (Courtesy Pasadena Museum of History Archives.)

PULL-OUT ON THE ARROYO SECO PARKWAY, 1948. On a rainy day in December, the roadway appears empty except for the parked car. The streaking lights, however, indicate a fair amount of traffic speeding into downtown. Highland Park and Pasadena are in the distance. (Courtesy *Herald-Examiner* Collection, Los Angeles Public Library.)

COMPLETED FIGUEROA TUNNELS. In 1931, a major public works project produced the tunnels under Elysian Park. This was the first major step in providing a non-stop thoroughfare for Route 66 from Pasadena to downtown Los Angeles using the meandering path of the Arroyo Seco. The art deco-inspired tunnels are among the most distinctive features of the road in California. However, today's speeds virtually deny us the opportunity to appreciate their design and construction. (Courtesy *Herald-Examiner* Collection, Los Angeles Public Library.)

"AMERICA'S MAIN STREET" BECOMING A FREEWAY. At least it's an attractive one! This photograph (c. 1980) on the high road into downtown through Elysian Park (the Figueroa Tunnels are through the hill to the left), shows what the population explosion and lack of mass transit options have done to "leisurely urban motoring." The Hill Street exit on the left flows directly into Chinatown, which continues its importance as a heritage resource in the current chapter of Route 66 history. (Courtesy Pasadena Museum of History Archives.)

"You must come out to see this beautiful ball park"

DODGER STADIUM. Built in 1962 along the Arroyo Seco Parkway (Pasadena Freeway) when the route was still in its glory days, Dodger Stadium certainly qualifies as a Route 66 corridor treasure. Designed by architect Ernie Praeger, it followed Walter O'Malley's vision to make the ballpark a signature Southern California attraction. For most of its life, Dodger Stadium was generally considered the most beautiful baseball park in the country. For the first three years, the ballpark was called Chavez Ravine, and the Dodgers shared the field with the Angels. It was an instant hit, and over the years more than 115 million fans have watched Dodgers at the stadium. This shot is from a souvenir placard for the 1963 World Series. (Courtesy Los Angeles Dodgers.)

DODGERS CELEBRATE THIRD STRAIGHT VICTORY IN 1963 SERIES. Don Drysdale had just shutout the Yankees, 1-0, in Game 3 against Jim Bouton. Game 4 completed the sweep when Sandy Koufax pitched a six-hit, 2-1 series capper. In two series starts, Koufax struck out 23 batters, including a single-game record of 15 in the series opener at Yankee Stadium. (Courtesy Los Angeles Dodgers.)

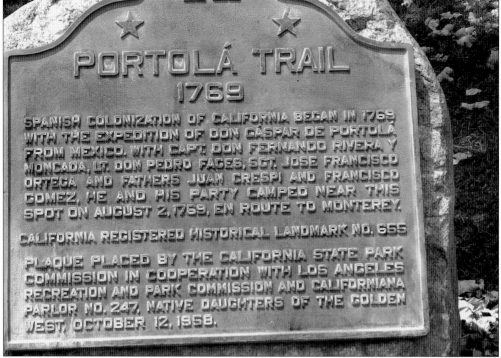

PORTOLA TRAIL MEMORIAL. At the west end of the Buena Vista Bridge, not more than 50 feet from Route 66, is this plaque placed near the site where Gaspar de Portola and his exploration party camped on their way to Monterey. (Courtesy Glen Duncan, California Route 66 Preservation Foundation.)

NORTH BROADWAY BRIDGE (BUENA VISTA VIADUCT). Intended to be seen by rail passengers traveling along the Los Angeles riverbed below and from Elysian Park on the north, this structure was designed by Alfred F. Rosenblum in 1911. It featured hexagonal handrail balusters, pedestrian viewing bays, and 37-foot-tall paired Ionic entrance columns topped by Doric entablature. The structure lost much of its ornament in the 1930s, but was seismically retrofitted and historically restored in 1997. (Courtesy Jeffrey Samudio and Portia Lee, and the Security Pacific Collection, Los Angeles Public Library.)

Six

Los Angeles
Metropolis

**1927 L.A. *Dealer-Herald*
Announcing Tourism Boom.**
Just a year after Route 66 is
inaugurated, the *Dealer-Herald*,
aimed at retailers, describes
a flood of 400,000 tourists in
Los Angeles. The chamber of
commerce is credited with strong
publicity efforts to build and
sustain the boom. After the early
days of unvarnished hyperbole
and California booster-ism
when railroads and hotels hired
accomplished artists to portray
and glorify the beauty of the
region's mountains, beaches,
deserts, and agricultural bounty,
the die was cast. With a new all-
weather highway from America's
heartland and the not-so-subtle
assistance of the burgeoning film
industry, Southern California
tourism became almost self-
sustaining. (Courtesy Security
Pacific Collection, Los Angeles
Public Library.)

NEW CHINATOWN, 1939. When construction began on Union Station in 1933, the old Chinatown was relocated several blocks north, along the Broadway Route 66 alignment. Although bypassed by Route 66 soon after, Chinatown has been within "spittin' distance" of the road and a major attraction to travelers ever since. (Courtesy Shades of L.A. Archives, Los Angeles Public Library.)

CHINATOWN GATEWAY. Recently installed, the dragon gate arches over Broadway. Behind us, as we look north from Cesar Chavez, is downtown L.A. Up Broadway is the new Chinatown, transplanted in 1933 from its former location in the area around Union Station to this site along Route 66. A little more than two years later, the road bypassed Chinatown, but the Hill Street off-ramp of the Arroyo Seco Parkway provided direct access to this popular tourist destination. (Courtesy Glen Duncan, California Route 66 Preservation Foundation.)

NORTH BROADWAY AND SUNSET, 1929. This is the intersection as it appeared two years before Broadway was widened. The entire hill was removed and the Broadway tunnel, in the center of the photograph, was demolished in 1931. (Courtesy Security Pacific Collection, Los Angeles Public Library.)

OLVERA STREET, 1959. This postcard shot shows Olvera Street shops with city hall in the background. Note the "Luncheon 75¢" sign on the restaurant. Olvera Street is part of the El Pueblo de Los Angeles National Register Historic District and includes an incredible concentration of significant landmarks depicting the early history of Los Angeles from early pueblo days. Olvera Street itself has been a major downtown tourist attraction since at least the early 1930s. (Courtesy Security Pacific Collection, Los Angeles Public Library.)

UNION STATION, LOOKING WEST TOWARD CITY HALL. Built in 1939 by a consortium of leading Los Angeles architects headed by Donald B. Parkinson, the station comprises a group of one-story stucco buildings with tile roofs, dominated by a 135-foot observation and clock tower. It is a highly artistic rendering of Spanish Colonial Revival architecture with a Moderne sensibility. The handsome interior has a 52-foot ceiling, marble floors, tall, arched windows, and superb California tile ornamentation. (Courtesy Security Pacific Collection, Los Angeles Public Library.)

SOLDIER LEAVING FOR WAR, 1941. Across Alameda from Olvera Street at Union Station on March 11, 1941, this photograph captures a brief moment in the lives of Pvt. Joe Sunseri and his girl, Alma Teresi, as he ships out. With war declared later that year, he would see duty in World War II. Military buildup from 1939 to 1945, the war, troop training, housing, and ordnance thrust Route 66 into a new and vital role in the lives of people across the country and particularly in Southern California. (Courtesy *Herald Examiner* Collection, Los Angeles Public Library.)

LOS ANGELES CIVIC CENTER IN EARLY ROUTE 66 DAYS. This picture was taken from the new city hall on Broadway, sometime between 1928, when it was occupied, and 1932, when the old courthouse on Spring Street (center of photograph) was demolished. The courthouse is flanked on the left by the Hall of Records and on the right by the Hall of Justice (now under restoration). The old 1888 Romanesque Revival city hall (not pictured) at Broadway and Second was demolished in 1928 after a spirited curbside auction of its furnishings. (Courtesy Security Pacific Collection, Los Angeles Public Library.)

LOS ANGELES TIMES **BUILDING, BROADWAY AND FIRST STREET.** The castellated Romanesque Revival building was where the *Los Angeles Times* called home when the road passed by in 1926. (Courtesy Security Pacific Collection, Los Angeles Public Library.)

LOS ANGELES THEATER. This view of the original marquee and facade depicts perhaps the grandest of all Broadway theaters. It was built in 1930–1931 and designed by architect Charles Lee. In the 1920s and 1930s, movie-going was an almost magical experience and movie palaces such as the Los Angeles, Orpheum, and Mayan, all here on Broadway, and the Chinese and Egyptian in Hollywood as well as the Rialto on Route 66 in South Pasadena were part of the show. Opulence and exotica of the theaters, particularly the interiors, are as much a part of our rich cinema heritage as the films that played in them. (Courtesy Security Pacific Collection, Los Angeles Public Library.)

SCHABER'S CAFETERIA, C. 1940. Several elaborate cafeterias thrived in the booming theater and shopping district near the original terminus of Route 66 at Seventh and Broadway. Cliftons's exotically themed establishments were undoubtedly the best known and greatest tourist attractions. The two-story Schaber's Cafeteria, at 610 South Broadway, relied more on opulence than kitsch in attracting motorists and pedestrians. (Courtesy Security Pacific Collection, Los Angeles Public Library.)

BROADWAY AND SEVENTH—END OF THE HISTORIC ALIGNMENT. This intersection between Loewe's State Theater and the Los Angeles Theater was the official terminus of Route 66 until the mid-1930s, when the route was extended to Santa Monica. The Broadway Theater District is listed on the National Register of Historic Places and the Los Angeles Conservancy offers a very popular annual June/July program of vintage films in restored theaters such as the Los Angeles and Orpheum. The Conservancy and California Route 66 Preservation Foundation have also placed signage on the southwest corner of the intersection, commemorating the original end of the road. (Courtesy Security Pacific Collection, Los Angeles Public Library.)

UNITED ARTISTS THEATER, 1929. This night view of the United Artists flagship theater marquee and box office on Broadway was near the end of the road from 1926–1936. Obviously the term "all talk" meant something different in 1929 than today, or Douglas Fairbanks and Mary Pickford would never have ascended to the pinnacle of the film stardom they rightfully achieved. (Courtesy Security Pacific Collection, Los Angeles Public Library.)

ORPHEUM THEATER. A block south stood the Orpheum, a premiere vaudeville and movie palace that has been lovingly restored. The Orpheum and Los Angeles theaters are now two of the most popular venues for the L.A. Conservancy's annual "Last Remaining Seats" vintage film screening program. (Courtesy Route 66 Corridor Preservation Program, National Park Service.)

1932 OLYMPICS. The 1932 Olympiad brought people from all over the world to Los Angeles and a good number undoubtedly came via "America's Main Street." This picture shows Los Angeles's Fairfax High grad "Dainty" Dorothy Poynton winning the platform diving event. She repeated the feat four years later in Berlin. (Courtesy Security Pacific Collection, Los Angeles Public Library.)

"WE LIKE IKE." In October 1958, an estimated 7,000 people jammed the street near the famous corner of Seventh and Broadway to show their support. This was after the road officially bypassed downtown on its way to Santa Monica. But having Pres. Eisenhower celebrated at the old Route 66 terminus is especially poignant in that he is generally credited with pushing for and inaugurating the Interstate Highway System that made Route 66 "obsolete." However, unlike the old adage that "old soldiers never die; they just fade away," public sentiment does not seem to be letting Route 66 fade away at all. (Courtesy Security Pacific Collection, Los Angeles Public Library.)

L.A. NIGHTLIFE DIVERSITY, 1950S. West Coast Jazz played an important role in Los Angeles and national culture for several decades in the mid-20th century and was a significant attraction to tourists and a burgeoning westward population migration. This picture captures the vitality of the local nightclub scene as Billie Raener, a noted journalist with the *Amsterdam News* (New York City) dances with Howard Allen. (Courtesy Shades of L.A. Archives, Los Angeles Public Library.)

PREHISTORIC MAMMALS AT THE LABREA TAR PITS, 1970S. Here are life size models of the animals whose bones were found trapped in the tar. They stand beside, and in, the modern tar pit located on Wilshire Boulevard's Miracle Mile. On the far side of the pit is a section of the Los Angeles County Art Museum and to the left is the Mutual Benefit Life building. (Courtesy Security Pacific Collection, Los Angeles Public Library.)

TWO YOUNG SWAINS AT KNOTT'S BERRY FARM. In the 1940s, Walter Knott had begun building a somewhat different theme park in Buena Park, based on his fascination with the old west. It has been a hit with Route 66ers ever since. In this 1961 snapshot, Freddy Rubio and Geraldo Village have sidled up to dance hall girls Cecelia and Marilyn, easily the two most photographed women in the park. (Courtesy Shades of L.A. Archives, Los Angeles Public Library.)

WATTS TOWERS, C. 1972. The internationally acclaimed artistic expression of Italian immigrant artist-builder Simon Rodia, the towers were designated a Los Angeles Landmark in 1963. Located at 1765 107th Street in Watts, the remarkable towers are about eight miles due south of the road's downtown path, but continue to draw 66ers and other visitors from all over the world. (Courtesy Pasadena Museum of History Archives.)

JAPANESE AMERICANS AT DISNEYLAND. With easy freeway access from downtown L.A., Walt Disney's new theme park became a prime destination, beginning in 1955, for Route 66ers from all over the country. For many, it was a big motivation for making the trip at all. Disney had essentially invented a new form of family entertainment. Here, in 1958, Hisataro and Sugi Kiriyama pose with their family in front of Sleeping Beauty Castle, a favorite "Kodak moment" location. (Courtesy Shades of L.A. Archives, Los Angeles Public Library.)

HERBERT'S DRIVE-IN, 1940S. Architect Wayne McAlister designed a raft of these circular Streamline Moderne drive-in restaurants all around Los Angeles. At the southeast corner of Beverly and Fairfax, a few blocks south of the Route 66 corridor, this Herbert's had the typical neon-ringed roofline and advertising pylon. (Courtesy Security Pacific Collection, Los Angeles Public Library.)

DRIVE-THRU CAR WASH, C. 1939. This is a typical drive-through car wash of the late 1930s and 1940s that abounded along Route 66 in Los Angeles. The spiffy white Studebaker sports a 1939 license plate. The car under the canopy is a Graham. (Courtesy Security Pacific Collection, Los Angeles Public Library.)

BOB'S BIG BOY, TOLUCA LAKE. Although not even close to a Route 66 alignment, this famous shot of a typical teen-age drive-in hang-out of the 1950s has become a classic and represents dozens, if not hundreds of similar sites along California Route 66, where waiters and waitresses served people eating in their cars. (Courtesy *Hollywood Citizen-News* Collection, Los Angeles Public Library.)

JENSEN'S RECREATION CENTER. This landmark animated bowling sign has been restored and often lights up the Sunset Boulevard–Silver Lake area. The attractive building is also essentially intact, although no longer operated as a recreation center. (Courtesy Glen Duncan, California Route 66 Preservation Foundation.)

JAY'S BURGERS. On Santa Monica Boulevard and Virgil, just west of Sunset Junction, Jay's Burgers appears to be dodging the wrecking ball as property around it is being developed. Let's hope this popular roadside amenity continues to be spared and reopens. (Courtesy Glen Duncan, California Route 66 Preservation Foundation.)

Seven

The Hollywood Experience

Hollywood, c. 1909, with Route 66 in Its Future. This is what Hollywood looked like at the corner of Santa Monica Boulevard and Highland Avenue perhaps a decade and a half before the Mother Road took this way out to Santa Monica. Essentially residential, with a Pacific Electric trolley running down the middle of the street, this photograph looks back northeast from the intersection. (Courtesy Security Pacific Collection, Los Angeles Public Library.)

ONE OF THE WORLD'S FAMOUS INTERSECTIONS. Few tourists back in Hollywood's glory years would pass up the opportunity to visit Hollywood and Vine. Visible near the center of the picture is the Hollywood Brown Derby sign atop this most famous of the Brown Derby restaurants, where celebrities truly outnumbered tourists and autograph seekers. The corner is now called Bob Hope Square, and is part of the Hollywood Boulevard National Register Historic District. (Courtesy Security Pacific Collection, Los Angeles Public Library.)

"GET YOUR KICKS." Hardly a block up Vine Street from Hollywood Boulevard is the iconic Capitol Records building, resembling a stack of LPs. It was Capitol that released the King Cole Trio's recording of Bobby Troupe's "(Get Your Kicks on) Route 66." Where two decades earlier in *Travels with Charley* and *The Grapes of Wrath*, Steinbeck had dramatized cultural impacts, "Get Your Kicks" set America's heart free. Now recorded by more than two hundred artists, Troupe's song has, among other things, put a lot of cars on the road. (Courtesy Route 66 Corridor Preservation Program, National Park Service, and Victorville Route 66 Museum.)

BOB HOPE AND FRIENDS. Almost everyone's fascination in Los Angeles turns to thoughts of stars. And here are two of the biggest in the 1950s at the 1952 annual police show at the Shrine Auditorium. A near capacity crowd of 5,000 watched Bob warn Chief William Parker not to get fresh as he pins an LAPD shield on actress Jane Russell. (Courtesy *Herald-Examiner* Collection, Los Angeles Public Library.)

GRAUMAN'S CHINESE THEATER OPENING. Movie fans crowd Hollywood Boulevard in front of Grauman's Chinese Theater. This group of thousands came in 1944 for the premiere of *Winged Victory*, which included a parade of stars and celebrities. (Courtesy *Herald-Examiner* Collection, Los Angeles Public Library.)

DORSEY AT PALLADIUM, 1940s. The Swing era was in full bloom during the war years as the Los Angeles area population swelled with servicemen's families and aircraft workers. Tommy Dorsey was at or near the top of the heap in popularity and this event at the world-famous Palladium played to a packed house. (Courtesy *Herald-Examiner* Collection, Los Angeles Public Library.)

HOLLYWOOD BOWL, 1931. The bowl has undergone many renovations over the years to improve acoustics and accommodations. Lots of architects have had a hand in its design, beginning with Lloyd Wright from 1924–1928, Myron Hunt in 1926, Allied Architects in 1931, Frank Gehry in 1982, and Hodgetts and Fung in 2004. This iteration in the early 1930s predated the tiered band shell appearance featured on countless postcard images. (Courtesy Shades of L.A. Archives, Los Angeles Public Library.)

ACADEMY AWARDS, PANTAGES. The 24th annual Academy Awards on March 22, 1952, sees Hollywood Boulevard jammed with cars bringing stars to the entrance. Sidewalks, special bleachers, and the entry bulge with fans, including the usual battalion of autograph hunters. The Pantages was built in 1929 in an exuberant art deco style. Badly damaged in the 1994 Northridge earthquake, it has been faithfully restored. (Courtesy Los Angeles Public Library.)

GRIFFITH PARK OBSERVATORY. This 1935 PWA Classical Moderne structure on the mid slope of Mount Hollywood is an excellent achievement in reinforced concrete. It was designed by John C. Austin and F. M. Ashley. (Courtesy Security Pacific Collection, Los Angeles Public Library.)

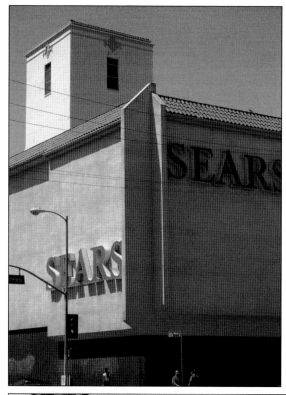

SEARS, HOLLYWOOD. The Mission Revival Department Store is still an anchor of the neighborhood, but not nearly the regional shopping magnet of the Route 66 heydays of the 1940s through the 1960s. Virtually everything but the tower has been substantially altered, but lifting ones eyes reveals a glimpse of past glory. (Courtesy Glen Duncan, California Route 66 Preservation Foundation.)

GHOST TOWN AT UNIVERSAL, 1939. Universal Studios has developed into one of Southern California's most popular tourist attractions. Along this famous street, the roaring life of the colorful West has been featured in hundreds of thrilling films shown around the world. Practically every big western hero in motion pictures got his start here or played his greatest role here. (Courtesy Security Pacific Collection, Los Angeles Public Library.)

GOLDWYN STUDIOS. THE Exterior of the Samuel Goldwyn Studios at the corner of Santa Monica Boulevard and Formosa Avenue is seen in the 1940s. At left is the Red Post Cafe, which later became the Formosa Cafe. (Courtesy Security Pacific Collection, Los Angeles Public Library.)

FORMOSA CAFE. On the site of the old Red Post Cafe, the Formosa has been a Hollywood mainstay for many years. A 1902 red trolley car still serves as the Star Dining Room. (Courtesy Glen Duncan, California Route 66 Preservation Foundation.)

FARMER'S MARKET. This popular Los Angeles institution has been packing them in for over three quarters of a century. Founded and still owned by the same family, who struck oil in their cow pasture, the complex is an open-air market, intermixed with restaurants and specialty shops. It's like a drive-in food market of the 1930s that has grown with the times and changing tastes. (Courtesy Security Pacific Collection, Los Angeles Public Library.)

TWO GUYS, A CORVETTE, AND ROUTE 66. Right next door to Farmers Market, at Beverly and Fairfax, is CBS Television City. The CBS-TV drama of the 1960s, *Route 66*, took road awareness and enthusiasm to a new level. (Courtesy the Route 66 Corridor Preservation Program, National Park Service.)

SANTA MONICA BOULEVARD, WEST HOLLYWOOD. Over the last 30 years, this section of urban Route 66 is one of the most improved, but not obliterated, segments in the Los Angeles area. West Hollywood is one of the newest cities in Los Angeles County. It proudly supports lifestyle diversity and has a large and growing population of Russian immigrants. (Courtesy Glen Duncan, California Route 66 Preservation Foundation.)

IRV'S BURGERS, WEST HOLLYWOOD. Open since 1944, about eight years after the road came this way, Irv's has legions of fans fighting to preserve it. Escalating property values in the area are not making it easy, however. (Courtesy Glen Duncan, California Route 66 Preservation Foundation.)

CHP SPOT CHECKING. Trying to cope with the huge influx of holiday party seekers on Sunset Strip, Santa Monica Boulevard, and other nearby thoroughfares, the California Highway Patrol set up roadblocks in late December 1965. Through January 1, they checked for drunk drivers, mechanical defects, and disorderly conduct. This checkpoint was on the Strip near La Cienega. (Courtesy *Herald-Examiner* Collection, Los Angeles Public Library.)

DINING AT CIRO'S "ON THE STRIP." The Sunset Strip beckoned tourists in legendary numbers from the 1950s through the 1960s, and Ciro's was probably the most exclusive dining spot, particularly popular with the entertainment community. Here Mr. and Mrs. Dean Martin join in celebrating the upcoming marriage of Nancy Davis, left, to Ronald Reagan. This was the kind of scene the autograph seekers dreamt of, but few could afford the tab here. (Courtesy *Herald-Examiner* Collection, Los Angeles Public Library.)

Eight

BEVERLY HILLS TO THE OCEAN

BEVERLY GARDENS PARK. For a little over three miles in its course through Beverly Hills, the north side of Santa Monica Boulevard (Route 66) is a park. This fabulous cultural landscape is one of a kind on America's Main Street. Hats off to the City of Beverly Hills for maintaining and preserving the park. Will Rogers would have been proud. (Courtesy Glen Duncan, California Route 66 Preservation Foundation.)

WILL ROGERS, MAYOR OF BEVERLY HILLS, 1926. Perhaps no single human being in the long history of Route 66 was more closely associated with the road than Will Rogers. In fact, for many years it was most commonly known as the Will Rogers Highway. And the same year that Route 66 was officially commissioned, Will Rogers was elected mayor of Beverly Hills, California, arguably the most glamorous city along its eight-state swath across the United States. This is his victory celebration. (Courtesy Security Pacific Collection, Los Angeles Public Library.)

BEVERLY HILLS HOTEL PORTE COCHERE. The elegant Beverly Hills Hotel, designed in Mission Revival style by Elmer Gray, has remained one of the most famous stopover and meeting spots for the bicoastal entertainment industry since the early days of film. Most important people in film and television have at one time or another stayed, had breakfast, lunch, and dinner or met here. With a nifty 1936 Ford convertible out front, this 1937 photograph conveys the sense of exclusivity and privacy that the hotel worked so hard to maintain. (Courtesy Security Pacific Collection, Los Angeles Public Library.)

I. M. PEI'S CREATIVE ARTISTS AGENCY. Just a very short block away from the "Mother Road," on Little Santa Monica Boulevard, stands one of this master architect's finest buildings. CAA is one of the most influential talent agencies in the entertainment business, and this imposing structure absolutely commands a view for westbound Route 66 travelers. (Courtesy Glen Duncan, California Route 66 Preservation Foundation.)

SAMMY DAVIS JR. AT BEVERLY HILTON. This crap game at the Beverly Hilton at Santa Monica and Wilshire Boulevards would have been highly illegal if it were real. But as a scene for the film *Johnny Cool*, it was totally legit. Tragically, though, it was on Route 66, in Cajon Pass, on his way back from Las Vegas, that the popular entertainer was involved in a car accident that resulted in the loss of his left eye. (Courtesy *Herald-Examiner* Collection, Los Angeles Public Library.)

A ROUTE 66 IN THEIR FUTURE. Before there was a road, before there were streets, there were dreams. Plans in hand, the three men here examine an area to become Santa Monica Boulevard. Taken in 1922, this photograph shows a billboard announcing Westwood, now open. (Courtesy Security Pacific Collection, Los Angeles Public Library.)

DOLORES, OF "WE NEVER CLOSE" FAME. This site on Santa Monica Boulevard is the only remaining Dolores Restaurant; like Tiny Naylor's and DuPars, these hearty-food, slightly upscale coffee shops used to be all over L.A. Let's hope the missing "e" in "We Never Close" is not an omen and this one stays open! (Courtesy Glen Duncan, California Route 66 Preservation Foundation.)

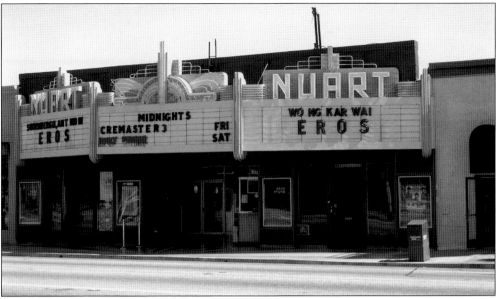

NUART THEATER, WEST L.A. The Nuart has been one the most successful and long-lived theaters in L.A., depending almost exclusively on alternative cinema; in the 1950s through the 1970s it showed primarily foreign films. Since then, a variety of foreign, independent, and offbeat films have continued to fill the bill. (Courtesy Glen Duncan, California Route 66 Preservation Foundation, and Security Pacific Collection.)

VILLAGE MOTEL, SANTA MONICA. Well-maintained and pristine, this 1930s motel enjoys a good roadside location in a nice neighborhood, midway between Beverly Hills and the beach. It is the only motel on Santa Monica Boulevard in Santa Monica and is a favorite of 66ers today. (Courtesy Glen Duncan, California Route 66 Preservation Foundation.)

DANCING THE CARES AWAY, 1942. On his last night out before leaving for the Army, defense worker Ben Abrams has a last fling at a Saturday night swing shift dance at Ocean Park. (Courtesy *Herald-Examiner* Collection, Los Angeles Public Library.)

WOMEN ANSWERING THE DRAFT AT DOUGLAS AIRCRAFT. With the war effort at full throttle, Marion Schultz joins thousands of women who assumed jobs vacated by men shipped off to the battlefront. She's an electric drill operator in the tail cone assembly of an A-20 Boston Bomber at Douglas, not far from the Mother Road. (Courtesy *Herald-Examiner* Collection, Los Angeles Public Library.)

PALISADES PARK, 1939. Although Route 66 never came here, the park, Santa Monica beach and pier below, and Ocean Park were all part of what we might call the "mythical" end of the road. Certainly, even before 1936 when Route 66 officially ended in downtown Los Angeles, most tourists would probably have come to the ocean and enjoyed a variety of entertainments and enticements offered in the vicinity. In this spirit, although inaccurate, a plaque commemorating this as the end of the fabled Will Rogers Highway has been placed in the park. (Courtesy Security Pacific Collection, Los Angeles Public Library.)

PACIFIC COAST HIGHWAY, 1937. This is the way PCH, then called the Roosevelt Highway, looked just a year after Route 66 came all the way to Santa Monica: very few cars and few homes restricting beach access. The big building at the left is the Marion Davies mansion; she was reportedly William Randolph Hearst's "main squeeze." (Courtesy Security Pacific Collection, Los Angeles Public Library.)

MUSCLE BEACH, SANTA MONICA, 1930s. Amazing feats of strength and acrobatics, and well-honed bodies, drew crowds from all across the country and sparked a fitness craze that continues to the present, although its devotees seem fewer and further between every year. (Courtesy Santa Monica Historical Society.)

OCEAN PARK PIER, 1930s. Another popular Santa Monica destination for travelers even before the road officially came this far, Ocean Park was a cornucopia of entertainment delights. (Courtesy Santa Monica Historical Society.)

NATIONAL 66 CONVENTION. Whether the primary inspiration was Will Rogers or U.S. Highway 66, this photograph from about 1940 demonstrates that the "Mother Road" was certainly part of civic consciousness in prewar Santa Monica. (Courtesy Paula Scott and the Santa Monica Library Image Archives; photograph by Adelbert Bartlett.)

ROUTE 66 BEAUTY CONTESTANTS ON SANTA MONICA BEACH, C. 1940. These enthusiasts for the "Will Rogers Highway" go to great lengths in Santa Monica. In this creative publicity photograph, bathing beauties plant a signpost in the sand, laying claim to the symbolic end of the road right here on the beach. Who's to argue? (Courtesy Santa Monica Historical Society.)

SANTA MONICA BEACH AND BEACH CLUBS, C. 1939. This view of Santa Monica beach shows crowds of people sun bathing or playing in the water. A volleyball game and several beach clubs can be seen in the background. (Courtesy Security Pacific Collection, Los Angeles Public Library.)

CHILDREN AT OCEAN PARK POSING AS MOVIE STARS. After a children's parade with floral floats in the 1930s, event organizers held a contest in which the kids dressed as movie stars. They seem to have the attitudes down pat. (Courtesy Security Pacific Collection, Los Angeles Public Library.)

END OF THE ROAD? Every road supposedly must come to an end (like most books); but this isn't it! Route 66 did not go up to, or onto, Santa Monica Pier. Likewise, it did not go onto the beach, despite what several pretty faces in a previous photograph may have exhorted you to think. However beguiling, it's a myth. Evidence documenting the road history (see next photograph) indicates that many have "mythed" the point. (Courtesy Route 66 Corridor Preservation Program, National Park Service.)

TO BE CONTINUED . . . Here at the busy intersection of Lincoln and Olympic Boulevards, Route 66 ceased to exist by converging into Pacific Coast Highway (Southbound 101). So the end of the road is not an end at all. Like 66ers in the various eras covered in foregoing photographs, you can continue any way you want. (Courtesy Vivian Davies.)

Museums and historical societies in many of the communities in the California Route 66 corridor have documentation and photographs relating to its impact on their communities. Each is easily accessible via the Internet and certainly worth the effort. None, however, focus on Route 66 to the extent found in the facilities listed below:

Barstow Route 66 "Mother Road" Museum
681 N. First Avenue
Barstow, CA 92311
(760) 255-1890

California Route 66 Museum
16825 D Street (Old Route 66)
Victorville, CA 92393
(760) 951-0436

Mojave Desert Heritage and Cultural Association
37198 Lanfair Road, G-15 near intersection of Goffs Road
Essex, CA 92332
(760) 733-4482

Mojave River Valley Museum
270 E. Virginia Way
Barstow, CA 92311
(760) 256-5452

Needles Regional Museum
923 Front Street
Needles, CA 92363
(760) 369-5678

In one way or another, with absolutely no effort to do so, author Glen Duncan has kept running into Route 66 since birth. He was born in Baxter Springs, Kansas, along its 13-mile route across the southeastern corner of the state. At three years of age he moved to Detroit, but most summers meant travel on Route 66 back to visit the grandparents. After graduating from Wayne State University, Glen went to work for Chevrolet's ad agency and was soon assigned to liaison duties on the *Route 66* television show, which included writing story synopses of scripts for client review. Years after relocating to Los Angeles, and two careers later, Glen married his wife, Pat, at the Casa de Adobe on Route 66. They now live in a 1914 Craftsman home, just three blocks from the historic alignment of Route 66 through South Pasadena. Largely due to his experience in historic preservation, including helping to save or restore properties along Route 66, Glen was asked to join the board of the California Route 66 Preservation Foundation. He now serves as vice president of the organization and is currently working on a survey of California Route 66 historic resources. He can be contacted via http://www.cart66pf.org.

BIBLIOGRAPHY

Adams, John Anthony. *Rialto*. Charleston, SC: Arcadia Publishing, 2004.

Apostal, Jane. *South Pasadena: A Centennial History*. South Pasadena, CA: South Pasadena Public Library, 1987.

Cataldo, Nick. *San Bernardino*. Charleston, SC: Arcadia Publishing, 2004.

Davies, Vivian, and Darin Kuna. *Guide to Historic Route 66 in California*. LaVerne, CA: California Route 66 Association, 1993.

Gebhard, David, and Robert Winter. *An Architectural Guidebook to Los Angeles*. Salt Lake City: Gibbs-Smith, 2003.

Hess, Alan. *Googie Redux: Ultramodern Roadside Architecture*. San Francisco: Chronicle Books, 2004.

Landers, John David. *Glendora*. Charleston, SC: Arcadia Publishing, 2004.

Langill, Mark. *Los Angeles Dodgers*. Charleston, SC: Arcadia Publishing, 2004.

Liebs, Chester. *Main Street to Miracle Mile: American Roadside Architecture*. Boston: Little Brown & Company, 1985.

Longstreth, Richard. *City Center to Regional Mall: Architecture, the Automobile, and Retailing in Los Angeles, 1920–1950*. Cambridge, MA: MIT Press, 1997.

Piotrowski, Scott R. *Finding the End of the Mother Road: Route 66 in Los Angeles County*. Pasadena, CA: 66 Productions, 2003.

Samudio, Jeff, and Portia Lee, Ph.D. *Los Angeles*. Charleston, SC: Arcadia Publishing, 2001.

Scott, Paula A. *Santa Monica: A History on the Edge*. Charleston, SC: Arcadia Publishing, 2004.

Wallis, Michael. *Route 66: The Mother Road*. New York: St. Martin's Press, 1990.

OTHER PUBLICATIONS AND PERIODICALS

"New Thoroughfare in Prospect between Pasadena and Los Angeles" and "Grade Crossing Dangers," *Touring Topics*, July 1911: 5–9.

"Club Sign System to Link Oceans," *Touring Topics*, 1914: 5–9.

"Western Link of Long Route Signed, *Touring Topics*, 1914: 5–9.

"Desert Driving Was Tough," *Westways*, December 1930: 60–61.